The Entrepreneur Magazine
Small Business Answer Book

The *Entrepreneur* Magazine Small Business Series

Published:

Forthcoming:

The Entrepreneur Magazine
Small Business Answer Book

Solutions to the

101

Most Common
Small Business Problems

Jim Schell

JOHN WILEY & SONS, INC.
New York • Chichester • Brisbane • Toronto • Singapore

Copyright © 1996 by Jim Schell
Published by John Wiley & Sons, Inc.

Library of Congress Cataloging-in-Publication Data:

Schell, Jim.
   The Entrepreneur magazine small business answer book : solutions
to the 101 most common small business problems / James Schell.
      p.   cm. — (Entrepreneur magazine small business series)
   Includes bibliographical references.
   ISBN 0-471-14841-5 (cloth : alk. paper). — ISBN 0-471-14842-3
(paper : alk. paper)
   1. Small business—Management.   I. Title.   II. Series.
HD62.7.S328   1996
658.02'2—dc20   95-53200

Printed in the United States of America
10 9 8 7 6 5 4 3 2 1

To Mary. We've seen it all.

Preface

Today is the age of the new entrepreneur. Every year, 750,000 of us enter the small business fray. Some come toting sophisticated business plans, state-of-the-art financing packages, and experienced management teams. Others come bearing little more than a blueprint, a savings account, and a long-festering dream. Some march into this career armed with graduate degrees in small business, others shuffle in with no previous business experience. There are no entrance exams in this vocation—entrepreneurs come from everywhere.

Yet, though our backgrounds may be different, every entrepreneur has two things in common. The first is that we're all embarking on a multifaceted and demanding career that poses a myriad of head-scratching questions. The second? You have to have been there to know how to answer those questions. And most entrepreneurs haven't.

Enter this book. You are about to be treated to 101 answers to the 101 questions the new entrepreneur will most likely ask. These answers encompass everything a small business owner and operator needs to know: from the start-up to the operation of an ongoing business; from an inside look at the species *entrepreneur* to how to manage employees; from the specifics of locating financing to the theories of *gamebreaking insights*. Whatever is needed to survive this roller coaster career, all can be found in the following pages.

The Entrepreneur Magazine Small Business Answer Book, incidentally, is not to be confused with *Gone with the Wind.* It should not be read from cover to cover and filed away in the archives somewhere to gather dust. Rather, it should be placed in plain view on the entrepreneur's desk top, to be referred to when questions arise—which won't be long, if you're anything like the rest of us.

Yes, questions *will* arise because this is a befuddling profession, especially for those who come trailing big business backgrounds. Remember, this small business gig is a lonely one. There are no legal departments to point out our judicial options, no human resource departments to resolve our personnel issues, no CFOs to call upon when our accounting questions arise. We're it. We either make the call or the call doesn't get made.

A quick disclaimer here. Yesterday's entrepreneurs were nuts and bolts kind of folks. Thus the answers they demanded were nuts and bolts, too; their primary goals were the *hows* of running a business. Meanwhile, today's successful entrepreneur must be as well versed in the *whys* of creating a small business as he is in the *hows*. As a result, the reader will find a sprinkling of theory midst the downpour of specifics presented herein. Yesterday's successful entrepreneurs will understand why.

What are my qualifications to answer these 101 questions? I've been there. Done them all. Answered each of these questions on more occasions than I'd care to admit. I was a bootstrapping entrepreneur (started my own business from scratch) four times over a 22-year career—created four successful small businesses, with the fourth and final business growing to $25 million in sales and 200 employees.

Over the course of those 22 years I've seen and done it all, where a privately held small business is concerned anyway. I've experienced just about everything that can befall a small business owner including runaway success, heart-stopping cash flow problems, and the most deadly killer of them all, entrepreneurial burnout. I've made an impressive number of right moves and an equally impressive number of wrong moves. As a result, I've learned the dos and don'ts, the shoulda's and coulda's, and the yeas and nays of starting and managing a small business. And I've come to despise the time-honored trial-and-error system that is a part of every new entrepreneur's modus operandi.

My intent in writing this book? To destroy that trial-and-error system forever.

Make no mistake about it, this career is significantly more complex today than it was 25 years ago. But the rewards it offers are significantly more exciting, too. The sky now falls somewhere short of the limit, as Bill Gates, Ted Turner, and a host of yesterday's successful entrepreneurs continue to prove every day.

I'll admit the questions in the following pages are not unique. They are the same questions that every entrepreneur, male or female, private or public, successful or unsuccessful, has faced over our unpredictable careers. Bill Gates, Ted Turner, or your neighborhood grocery store owner, it matters not. Each of us has confronted them all.

It's the answers herein that are unique. As unique as the entrepreneurs who have taken advantage of them. Hopefully, this will include you.

Contents

PART VI: Culture   159

Questions

PART I

The Entrepreneur and Small Business

A number of common denominators define the successful entrepreneur and his or her successful small business. Something that makes the entrepreneurs who survive different from those who don't. Something that separates the small business that lands on its feet from the one that falls on its face.

Something that makes the *Microsoft*s out of the *mom and pops.*

Let's see what those somethings are. . . .

QUESTION 1

Q "What is an entrepreneur?"

A The dictionary defines an entrepreneur as "a person who organizes and manages a business undertaking, assuming the risk for the sake of the profit."

Baloney, risk and entrepreneurs have very little in common (see Question 86).

My definition of an entrepreneur is "a person who would rather trust the marketplace than the East Coast regional manager." The successful entrepreneurs I know would rather roll the dice themselves than have someone else roll the dice for them.

Other conceptions, or misconceptions, that people have about entrepreneurs include:

- Some say entrepreneurs are courageous. (They aren't. People who depend on East Cost regional managers for their livelihoods are the courageous ones.)
- Some say entrepreneurs make lousy employees. (They usually do.)
- Some say entrepreneurs are control freaks. (They usually are.)
- Some say entrepreneurs value growth more than security. (They'd better.)
- Some say entrepreneurs thrive on change. (Ditto above.)
- Some say entrepreneurs are workaholics. (They aren't. They may work long hours, but entrepreneurs work to achieve, while workaholics work to escape.)

Yes, entrepreneurs are people who have decided they can beat the marketplace themselves. Their reasons are varied and many . . .

they have a better mousetrap perhaps, or know of a better distribution system, or can assemble a better team. There is no limit to the dreams of entrepreneurs.

So, what does it take for us to become entrepreneurs?

Not much. Let's face it, we aren't talking about a close-knit community of well-trained, career-educated, finely tuned professionals here—just about any warm body can become an entrepreneur. A letterhead here, a fax machine there, and zap, zap—you're an entrepreneur. Deciding to become one is not the same as deciding to become an aeronautical engineer.

But what about a *successful* entrepreneur? Can anyone become one of these?

The answer is a resounding no.

Having *the dream* is not enough. We must also have the passion to accomplish the tasks required to fulfill that dream. And then we must be willing to make the commitment to accomplish those tasks. And finally we must be capable of achieving results: doing whatever it takes to turn those commitments into reality.

My intention is not to romanticize the entrepreneur. We certainly confuse debits with credits, wear socks that don't match, and forget anniversaries, just like everyone else. But make no mistake about it, this career is not for your basic accountant, payroll clerk, or government employee.

This career is for people who are driven to achieve.

QUESTION 2

Q "What is the difference between today's and yesterday's entrepreneur?"

A   Telecommunications, politics, and major league baseball are not the only career fields that have suffered through wrenching changes in the last twenty-five years. Entrepreneuring has, too.

Remember yesterday's entrepreneur? He or she of the sweat-stained armpits? In the cluttered office? Hunched over the ledgers in the wee hours of the morning? Who made all the decisions, called all the shots, and had his or her nose stuck permanently in every employee's business? Yesterday's entrepreneurs were the sweatshop kings and queens of the world, dictating the affairs of their companies the same way Archie Bunker dictated the affairs of his family. With the mouth and, when necessary, with the fist.

I should know. I was one.

How times have changed.

Yesterday's entrepreneur hung out a shingle, crossed his or her fingers, and waited for the customers to come. Today's successful entrepreneur prepares sophisticated business plans, researches the marketplace, and prepares a database on all potential customers. And *then* hangs out a shingle.

Yesterday's entrepreneur scribbled debits and credits in the general ledger, then totaled them frantically at month's end, only to turn them over to an accountant and sweat out the results. Today's successful entrepreneur enters data daily, lets the computer do the work, and pushes the print-out button on the last day of the month.

Yesterday's entrepreneur worked alone. (Where was there to go for help?) Today's successful entrepreneur subscribes to small business magazines, chats online with other small business owners, and listens to the advice of a board of advisors—between keeping in touch with a mentor.

Yesterday's entrepreneur issued orders, barked out commands, and directed the troops. Today's successful entrepreneur recognizes that employees are not the plodding marionettes small business employers once thought they were, but rather are talented people with skills, knowledge, and minds of their own. Today's successful entrepreneur runs his or her company as a democracy, not as a dictatorship.

What's more, not only has the mindset of today's successful entrepreneur changed, but the roles he or she plays has, too. No longer is the entrepreneur the number one worker; today he or she is the number one cheerleader. The entrepreneur's job isn't to *do* any more, but rather to provide an environment in which employees can *do.*

In days past, it was always the entrepreneur who was willing to work the hardest; who had the choicest location, location, location; who manufactured the best widget; who usually won. Yesterday's successful entrepreneurs were the bulldogs and the plow horses of the small business world.

No longer. Today it's the entrepreneur who is the most thoroughly prepared, who has the most information, and who recognizes that business success is no longer a solo journey. Today's successful entrepreneurs are the greyhounds and the quarter horses of the small business world.

And most of all, today's successful entrepreneurs are the trial-and-error avoiders—those people who learn their lessons from the trials and errors of others.

So, welcome to this book. May all my trials and errors be lessons for you.

QUESTION 3

Q "What is the number one determinant of the entrepreneur's success?"

A Recognizing that it is bad form to answer a question with a question, I'll do so anyway.

What do *you* think the number one determinant is?

Is it your employees? Your niche? Your location, location, location?

No, no, and no, no, no. The number one determinant of your success is you. The entrepreneur. The chief enchilada. The big kahuna. It's a fact, the decisions you make and the directions you take place you light years ahead of whatever the number two determinant is.

Sure, your team of employees is a make-it-or-break-it element of success. But, I ask you, who assembles that team in the first place? And sure, the niche is important, but I ask you, who determines it? And sure, location, location, location is important, but I ask you, who selects it? See what I mean? The entrepreneur is the source of every good decision made in the fledgling business—and every bad one, too.

There are no excuses for failure. None. Yes, bad luck befalls us all now and then, but good luck does, too. And yes, competitors attack, but they attack in every career field; this one is no exception. And yes, the economy ebbs and flows, but it ebbs and flows for our competitors, too. Every business has its ups and downs.

But what every business doesn't have is you. You're it, where your small business's survival is concerned. Your business will either live or die because of you.

There is no other way to answer this question. Everything that happens within your company starts, and ends, with you, the entrepreneur. The buck—good, bad, or indifferent—stops on your desk.

But, after all, isn't this the way you prefer it? Just think—no more supervisors, bosses, or East Coast regional managers.

Isn't that the reason you selected this career in the first place?

QUESTION

Q "What *is* the entrepreneur's favorite learning tool?"

A   Oh, brother, can I answer this one!

The entrepreneur's number one learning tool is trial and error. Good, old-fashioned, nineteenth-century, take-no-prisoners, trial and error.

Think about it. What other profession (politics excepted) makes the same old dusty mistakes, month after painful month? What other profession reinvents the same old medieval wheel, year after monotonous year? What other profession has the same grizzly failure rate, decade after fatal decade?

For instance, what if medical professionals learned their lessons the way we do? What would be the effect on their patients? How about lawyers, or bean counters, or our Fortune 500 big-business cousins? What would be the impact on our legal system, our accounting system, and our financial markets if trial and error was their number one learning tool?

Although trial and error is the world's finest teacher (its lessons last a lifetime . . . the good ones and the bad ones), it is also the most expensive one. Yes, we learn more from our mistakes than we do from our successes, but not in the quantity, or at the price, that we need. And yes, we are in a learning-by-doing profession, but what else could we have been learning and doing if we hadn't been so busy correcting our mistakes?

And don't tell me that trial and error goes with the entrepreneurial turf. Maybe it has in the past, but it won't for tomorrow's successful entrepreneurs. After all, there's nothing in the entrepreneurial oath that says we can't open our eyes, our ears, and our minds. There's nothing in that oath that says we can't learn from someone else's mistakes instead of our own.

Ironically, it isn't the entrepreneurial turf that's the problem. It's the folks who are trodding that turf.

That's us.

And it's our hard-headed independence that's bogging us down.

QUESTION 5

Q "What *should be* the entrepreneur's favorite learning tool?"

A Experience. As in, somebody else's.

I can promise you this. There is nothing new in the business of small business; everything that is happening today has happened before. Okay, so maybe today's happenings are taking a different form or adding a new twist when compared to what took place yesterday. But forms or twists aside, you are not the first small business owner to suffer a shortage of capital or to confront an employee who thinks he shouldn't be fired or to face an OSHA inspector. Someone has suffered that shortage, confronted that employee, or faced that OSHA inspector before.

And that someone has written, or is writing, about such subjects as capital shortages and firing employees and OSHA inspectors, along with every other small business crisis known to exist. Or that someone is traveling the countryside, talking about those crises. Or that someone is perched in the office next to yours, willing to talk about his or her experiences, if given the opportunity.

But we entrepreneurs have been too busy putting out our fires to listen to that someone. Or maybe we thought we had all the answers already. Or maybe we were just too independent to ask for help.

Enough of this lecture, you say. What are the options to learning by trial and error? Where can an entrepreneur find experienced help to avoid these problems?

Consider the following:

1. Taking a partner.
2. Finding a mentor.

3. Appointing a board of directors or a board of advisors (with outside members).
4. Hiring a consultant.
5. Networking with other entrepreneurs.
6. Joining trade associations and small business associations.
7. Taking advantage of the U.S. government's offerings.
8. Subscribing to small business magazines.
9. Seeking help on the Internet.
10. Requesting assistance from Fortune 500 companies, such as IBM, AT&T, the bigger banks, and the Big Six accounting firms, all of which have programs designed to help small businesses.

Have you taken advantage of any of these options? If not, why not?

We'll discuss most of these options in detail later in this book. Suffice it to say that the tools of experience are available, if you're willing to look for them.

And you'd better be. Trial and error as a small business management tool is on its way out.

QUESTION 6

Q "What is a small business?"

A Possibly the greatest thing about this country, aside from the fact that virtually any warm body can be elected president, is that virtually any warm body can also open a small business. There are no stipulations where age, gender, or IQ are involved. If Forrest Gump can do it, anybody can.

So 750,000 of us open small businesses every year. With a corresponding number of failures, sales, and retires, 750,000 of us also move on, leaving approximately 6,200,000 business owners plying our trade—or trading our ply—or whatever it is we do during our open-for-business hours.

For those of you who are turned on by statistics, here is a collection of small business data designed to make you absolutely delirious.

- The Small Business Administration (SBA) defines small business as any business with less than 500 employees.
- Of the United States' 6,200,000 small businesses, 5,400,000 employ less than 20 employees each.
- There are 10,000 *big businesses* in the U.S. with 500 to 1,000 employees, and 6,000 with more than 1,000 employees.
- Small businesses employ 72,000,000 people. (Never have so many people had so little clout.)
- Small business's annual payroll is $1.5 trillion; big business's, a paltry $5.5 billion.

- Of the 6,200,000 small businesses in the United States, 1,400,000 are growing at a rate of more than 15% per year.

Now that we have satisfied your hunger for statistics, here are some general characteristics of a typical small business.

- Things happen fast. (Things had better happen first, because that's the way our customers expect them to happen.)
- The customer is king.
- Things don't stay the same very long. Change comes quickly, and often.
- It's OK to be different, as long as the *different* employee contributes to the team. (After all, nonconformity is what got the founder into this business in the first place.)
- Creativity and risk taking are encouraged, and people who aren't afraid to make mistakes are welcome.
- Employers and employees must mind their expenses. Capital is finite.
- Profitability comes first and rewards later—after the cash is in the bank.
- The small business is a reflection of its owner. It believes what the owner believes and rejects what the owner rejects. It reflects the owner's personality.
- Most of all, a small business is an organism. It is born, it lives, and, too often, it dies. The entrepreneur is its heart; the employees, its blood.

Small business survivors are, for the most part, proud of these descriptions. They are what makes us different from the *Procter & Gambles*, the *General Motors*es, and the highway maintenance departments of the world. But, like everything else, there are trade-offs.

Small businesses don't have the same resources the big guys have. There is no endless supply of cash to throw at our problems. There is no infinite source of people to get the jobs done. Other limitations include:

- Less security (although this is changing).
- Lower pay scales, especially at the entry level.

- Fewer benefits.
- Less structure.
- A higher mortality rate.

But, for people who see challenges as opportunities, small business is where it's at. Small business is the future of America's economic growth.

QUESTION 7

Q "What is the number one cause of small business failure?"

A *You* give this question a try.

Is the number one cause of small business failure the lack of capital? How about poor hiring techniques? Or maybe the wrong niche? Lousy location? A lack of quality control?

Well?

Sorry, but no cigar. The above are all *symptoms* of failure, but not causes.

The number one cause of small business failure is the number one person making the decisions. You know who I'm talking about . . . the locked-in-his-office-with-his-problems-stacked-to-the-ceiling entrepreneur. Or, more specifically, the number one cause is that dreaded disease that inflicts entrepreneurs, causing them to spend the majority of their working life fighting fires in a vacuum.

The number one cause is *entrepreneurial loneliness* disease.

Think about it. There are no symptoms in existence that could wipe out an otherwise healthy small business if the entrepreneur recognizes them and acts quickly to eliminate them. Yet, because of our overactive independence genes, we choose not to search out the experience necessary to overcome those symptoms. We go through life without a mentor, without a board of directors, without learning the facts of business life from someone else. Resolutely we stand, individually we fall.

Yes, entrepreneurs, as discussed earlier, are the primary catalysts for success in small business.

But they are also the primary cause of its failure.

PART II

The Small Business Start-Up

When entrepreneurs make the decision to start up a small business, they aren't just starting up that business—they are creating a foundation for a bigger business. The niche they pick, the culture they establish, and the ethics and principles they espouse will be identifying characteristics for as long as the entrepreneurs and their companies are together.

That's why the start-up isn't just a *stage*.

The start-up is a forever.

.

QUESTION 8

Q "What are the most important elements of a start-up?"

A   Before answering this question, I'm assuming that the start-up chores necessary to opening a small business in this paper-mad world have been fulfilled—those no-brain-but-necessary chores, such as completing and filing articles of incorporation; fulfilling all the licensing requirements (local, state, and federal); keeping the federal taxing agencies happy (income, Social Security, excise, and unemployment); and satisfying all the state and local taxing agencies.

With that assumption in mind, here are the five most important elements of a start-up, the neglect of which is sure to propel your small business into the jaws of the great paper shredder in the sky.

ATTENTION TO DETAIL

There are a growing number of small business gurus who believe that the number one determinant of success in growing a business from start-up to maturity is attention to detail. Read Sam Walton's biography if you want to hear from one of them.

When details are neglected during the start-up stage, the following problems result:

- Those details add up—and up. Eventually, they are no longer details. They become roadblocks, then bottlenecks, then . . . .
- The neglect of details becomes a cultural issue. If the boss neglects details, the employees will, too. Soon the entrepreneur will have an entire company filled with employees frantically going about the task of neglecting details.

Details come in many sizes, shapes, and forms, and range from returning a supplier's phone call to finalizing a new hire's employment contract to filling out the warranty on the new computer. Details are not fun—by an entrepreneur's definition of fun, anyway—and most don't seem important at the time. But, invariably, those details come back to haunt their avoider, except that, when they return, they aren't details anymore. They are roadblocks. And bottlenecks. And . . . .

HEALTHY CULTURE DEVELOPMENT

Remember, entrepreneurs not only build businesses, they also develop cultures. If the entrepreneur shows up late for work, employees will assume they can, too. If the entrepreneur takes twenty-minute coffee breaks, employees will assume they can, too. And if the entrepreneur dips his hand in the cash register whenever he passes, the employees will, too.

The establishment of culture begins the entrepreneur's first day on the job. From the beginning, the entrepreneur sets the standards for the company's attitudes toward such critical matters as quality, service, and concern for the customer. These attitudes will be a part of the culture as long as the entrepreneur remains with the company. (For more on the subject of culture, see Questions 66 through 70.)

BUSINESS PLANNING

The business plan forces the entrepreneur to plan and prepare in advance. The more planning and preparation are put into the business plan, the better it will be. Also, the seeds for strategic planning are planted even before the business opens its doors.

Planning, as every successful entrepreneur has learned, is the antidote for bad luck. Without plenty of the former, expect more of the latter.

ADEQUATE CREDIT OR CAPITALIZATION

Too many small businesses, as a result of poor planning and faulty forecasting, don't ask their bank, shareholders, angels, friends, or relatives for enough cash. Then, when times get tight and the business needs an infusion of cash, guess what? The cupboards are bare.

The start-up lessons here? (1) Seek experienced help when determining your cash needs, (2) make sure you get enough cash the first time around, and (3) plan, plan, plan.

TEAM-ASSEMBLING RESPONSIBILITIES

You say you're too busy to follow up on the job applicant's references? Too busy to interview the applicant twice? Too busy to cross all the t's and dot all the i's of the detail-ridden hiring process?

You say you're too busy to train your new employees? Too busy to motivate them properly? Too busy to solve your employee's problems as you create an environment in which they can grow?

I say you're too busy to own a small business.

Running a small business isn't all dealing with customers, developing new products, and planning new strategies. Running a small business involves a myriad of organizing, training, and motivating (team-building) responsibilities that are just as essential to success, but not as much fun.

Team-building. A tedious task, to be sure, but one that, given adequate attention, will ensure plenty of companionship through the start-up stage and beyond. Neglect team-building and you are bound to have a long journey—alone.

QUESTION

Q "My idea is so good, why should I even consider a partner?"

A I know what you're thinking—partners can be a pain in the keister. And you're right. Small business's annals are filled with thousands of blood-curdling tales about the disagreements, fights, and messy divorces that result when partners don't get along. No question about it, partnerships are potential "disasterships," waiting to happen.

But . . .

Did you know that studies indicate partnerships outperform sole proprietorships by a substantial margin? It isn't even close, especially when the two partners have complementary skills. You're a salesnik? Find an operations type. You're an inventor? Find someone who can get the product on the shelves. You're a mover and shaker? Find someone who can count the beans that you've been moving and shaking.

So . . .

Search for a complementary partner. Then find a good lawyer, one who specializes in small business partnerships. Draw up an ironclad, airtight, cast-in-stone buy-sell agreement. Oh yes, and don't forget to talk to several successful partners who have gone the route before. Talk to several failed ones as well (you won't have any trouble finding either). Try to determine the conflicts that usually arise (unrealistic expectations are the number one killer of partnerships) and how the two of you can expect to resolve them. Understand going in that your ironclad, airtight, cast-in-stone buy-sell agreement is liable to be tested—by conflicting, nonfriendly parties.

Besides the increased opportunity for success, there are several other reasons why partnerships make sense.

- *Ease of formation.*   Partnerships are easier, and less expensive, to form than corporations (but not as easy, or as inexpensive, as sole proprietorships).
- *Additional capital.*   Two savings accounts are better than one. And two personal guarantees are better than one.
- *Additional problem-solving capability.*   Two minds are better than one.
- *Flexibility.*   One partner can go on vacation, while the other minds the store. Not so for sole proprietorships.
- *Less risk.*   Profits aren't the only thing partners share.

And one more thing, while on the subject of partnerships. Remember, when you take a partner, that it's like consummating a marriage . . . the two of you enter into a long-term relationship. Trust, respect, and the ability to communicate will ultimately determine the success or failure of the partnership—if they aren't around at the outset, the relationship is probably doomed.

So why all the fuss about partners if the chances for discord are so high?

Because, as someone once said (don't ask me who), "'Tis far better to have something to fight over than to have nothing at all."

QUESTION

Q "How important is the niche?"

A Everything being relative, not very.

I'm not suggesting that tomorrow you should go into the buggy whip business or open a speakeasy or build a drive-in movie theatre. Some niches are better than others.

And some niches are more forgiving than others, too. Come up with a new software idea, a new telecommunications tool, or a new multimedia concept, and (assuming ample financing) you'll have room to make a few early mistakes. However, come up with a new restaurant concept or a new retail clothing store or a new athletic shoe, and, beware—the margin for error is thin.

When compared to the three other key factors that determine the success or failure of a small business, the niche finishes a weak fourth. Those three factors are:

1. The quality of the entrepreneur. (We've discussed this one in answer to Question 3.)
2. The quality of the entrepreneur's team. (See Question 32.)
3. The quality of the financing package. (I don't care how good the product or service is, if there isn't enough capital to get it to the marketplace, it won't sell.)

What does all this mean to you? It means you may have the greatest idea since velcro, the greatest concept since post-its, and the greatest product since the fax, but those ideas, concepts, and products won't mean "diddley squat" if you don't first have your people and financing resources in place.

With this disclaimer in mind, it is important that the entrepreneur selects a niche that he or she enjoys and can afford. A personal experience of mine illustrates both.

I chose my first business, the retail and wholesale sporting goods industry, not because I saw a tremendous profit potential in it (I didn't) or because no one else was selling sporting goods at the time (plenty were), but because I enjoyed participating in sports and wanted to stay involved. What better way, I surmised, than by being in a related business. (I suspect Colonel Sanders chose his niche for the same reason.)

As it turned out, selling sporting goods was a tough way to make a living because a lot of people enjoyed sports; thus, competition was everywhere. Nevertheless, I survived, even prospered, because I enjoyed every minute of those up-and-down years, even the unprofitable ones. Had I been in, for instance, the plumbing fixtures business, I would have been history.

One problem, however. Success in the sporting goods industry meant having a prime location, shelves stocked with inventory, and, on the wholesale side of the business at least, the associated costs of carrying accounts receivable. Meeting these conditions required borrowing money, which, for an undercapitalized entrepreneur like me, also meant diluting ownership and paying interest.

If I had it to do all over again, I'd still pick the sporting goods business, thus fulfilling the *enjoyment* requirement, but I'd get into the manufacturer's rep side instead, thereby fulfilling the *affordable* requirement. (Manufacturer's reps need no inventory, own no real estate, and carry few receivables.) The perfect world.

The same criteria should apply to you. Find a niche that you like and one you can afford. Then immerse yourself in it and, keep your eyes open.

Perhaps an even better niche will appear.

QUESTION 11

Q "Why do I need a business plan?"

A Maybe you don't. For instance, you don't need a business plan if:

- You have more money than the Rockefellers and you'll never have to worry about cash, no matter what happens to that little old business of yours. Or . . .
- You know exactly where you're going and don't care if anyone else does. Or . . .
- You haven't the foggiest idea where you're going and couldn't care less.

However, the rest of us do need a business plan. In order of importance, a business plan functions as:

1. *A sales tool.* The number one use of a business plan is as a sales tool. It serves as a prospectus, an invitation to invest or to provide a loan, and, at the same time, the first official presentation to the outside world of the kind of product or service the preparer will be offering. Prospective bankers or investors will initially judge the entrepreneur's abilities and his or her chances for success on the quality of the business plan.

    Surprisingly, the strategies contained in the business plan are not as important to knowledgeable bankers and investors as is its quality and professionalism. They know that events will dictate changes in those strategies, and that what *is* important is the entrepreneur's ability to manage those changes.

    Experience has taught them, it's the jockey that wins the race, not the horse.

2. *An exercise in strategic planning and business logistics.*   Assembling the business plan is the entrepreneur's first official exercise in strategic planning and business logistics. It is an exercise that too many of us action-oriented entrepreneurs tend to overlook, both during the start-up stage of our business, and later on, when we're in the heat of the battle.

   And yet, even where these elements of strategy and logistics are concerned, it isn't the plan itself that is of greatest importance.

   It's the process of drafting the plan that counts.

3. *A barometer and a scorecard.*   A business plan sets goals—Written goals, published goals, goals for the world to see. Goals that publicly state the entrepreneur's intentions.

   Subsequent financial statements will indicate progress toward achieving those goals. Documented progress for the world to see.

   Just think—goals in writing, to be followed by our progress measured publicly.

   The ultimate word in accountability.

QUESTION 12

Q "What are the most important elements of the business plan?"

A Business plans come in a variety of shapes and forms, depending on the size of the deal, the needs of the lender, and the sophistication of the entrepreneur. Entire books have been written on the subject of business plans, and even computer software is available to lead the first time business plan developer through the process. The entrepreneur who is seeking serious financing should not cut corners when developing a business plan. Plenty of information is available.

This section is intended for overview only. After reviewing this chapter, the entrepreneur in search of capital should either (a) read one of the many books written specifically about business plans (all the major accounting firms have free business planning brochures available to the public); (b) purchase some business planning software; (c) ask his or her accountant, lawyer, or SBA counselor for a copy of someone's already-successful business plan; or (d) hire a consultant (business plan consultants can be found in most major cities) to assist in developing the plan.

The following are the important elements that should be included in every business plan.

THE COMPANY

1. *Management.* Include complete biographical sketches of you and your key employees. The reader will be looking for specific

accomplishments, not just job history. Also include a prospective organization chart, along with a management philosophy statement indicating how you will be managing your team.

Remember, potential investors and/or creditors look first for quality and experience in you and your team members. As discussed in Question 11, the players are more important to a small business's success than any other aspect of the plan. Be thorough, objective, and accurate when describing the players.

2. *Mission.*   Include a mission statement. (If you don't have one, you should. See Question 14.)
3. *Recruitment.*   Explain how and where you intend to find employees.
4. *Training.*   Describe the training that will be provided for your existing team and your new hires.
5. *Organization.*   Indicate the type of organization you've chosen (Subchapter S? C Corp? Partnership? Sole proprietorship?) and why.
6. *Location.*   Include a description of all offices and warehouse and physical facilities.

THE SERVICE OR PRODUCT

What is your service or product? What are its benefits? What makes it special? How it will be manufactured, produced, or procured? What will be the cost and projected selling price? How about warranties, guarantees, and ongoing service? Answer these questions and include information about your product or service history, along with everything applicable to patents, trademarks, or copyrights (yours or someone else's).

THE MARKET

1. *The industry.*   Provide an industry overview. How big is your market? What is your market's growth prospects? How competitive is the marketplace? How profitable are the major players?
2. *The customers.*   Identify the individual groups or companies you will target as customers. What similar products/services are they

purchasing now? Why would they seriously consider purchasing your product? Who in each company would be doing the actual buying? And most importantly, which of your customer's needs will your product or service fulfill?

3. *The competition.*   List your competitors. What are their approximate market shares? What are their strengths and weaknesses?

DISTRIBUTION

What will be your approach to selling the product? Your own in-house sales force? Factory reps? Mail order? Catalog? Include the whys, as well as the hows. Also, describe your marketing, advertising, and promotional plans in this section.

Distribution (sales and marketing) is second only to the quality of the team when it comes to determining success. This section of the business plan will be of primary importance to sophisticated investors or creditors.

FINANCIAL

1. *Financial organization.*   Decide how much of your own money you are investing. What are you looking for, debt or equity? How much additional capital do you need? Where you are seeking equity, who are the other shareholders? What are their ownership percentages? What are their exit provisions?

2. *Financial projections.*   Include projected profit and loss statements and balance sheets for at least three, and no more than five years. Make them as realistic as possible—sophisticated investors and/or creditors will quickly recognize projections that are padded or overoptimistic. (Once they perceive this to be the case, the interview is over.)

3. *Compensation.*   How will you and your key employees be compensated? Include stock options, bonus plans, and perks.

RISKS AND REWARDS

1. *Risks.*   What are they? Shrinking markets? Aggressive competitors? Interest rates? Government policies? New technologies? Be

blunt and be frank; every new venture has a risk. The business plan reader is looking for honesty here.

2. *Rewards.*   Include expectations regarding dividends, loan repayment, reinvestment of profits, expansion, public offerings, and so on.

DETAILS

This is the "dotting of the i's and crossing of the t's" section. The *attention to details* section. Don't overlook its importance. If the potential investor/creditor is one of those Sam Walton-type folks who believe that it's attention to detail that makes or breaks the entrepreneur, he or she will scour this section with a fine-toothed comb.

Include such details as legal and accounting firms, description of leases, prospective vendors, required licenses and/or agreements, product development needs, and pertinent personnel issues.

Finally, remember that your business plan reflects directly on you. You are about to be judged as to your professionalism and capability to manage a business, often by people, or a committee of people, who will never meet you face-to-face.

With this thought in mind, ask yourself this question, once you've finished assembling your business plan:

"Does this reflect the way I want to be perceived?"

If it does, you've done everything you possibly can.

If it doesn't, it's back to the drawing board.

QUESTION 13

Q *"Visions, missions, and goals. What good are they?"*

A Not much.

Not much, that is, if there's only us in our small business. In which case those visions, missions, and goals can remain locked in our pointed little heads. After all, we know where we're going and how we're going to get there. Who else needs to be in on the secret?

But as soon as we've hired our first employee, all bets are off. That's because employees aren't privy to what's inside of our pointed little heads until we open up to them. We must let them know what's going on inside, by publicly apprising them of our visions, missions, and goals.

Our visions, missions, and goals need to be shared. After all, mailroom employees, accounting clerks, and salespeople need visions, missions, and goals in their working life, too. Better for them to be pursuing ours than someone else's. Better for us all to be chasing a common dream, down a common road, with common objectives.

Specifically, here's what we need to share.

- *Vision.* Our employees need to know the dream in the back of our head. They need to know where they are ultimately bound. They need a destination.

  Do visions change? You bet your sweet dreams they do. Not too often, hopefully, because most people (entrepreneurs excluded) need some degree of consistency in their lives. Change is not an aphrodisiac for most employees, as it is with us.

- *Mission.* Mission gives direction to the entrepreneur's vision. The mission statement is a public affirmation of what the company is, not only for the employees to know, but for the rest of the world, too. It is a short, sound-bite, paragraph or two describing what the company is, why it's in business, and what makes it different from the rest

- *Goals.*   We're talking specifics here. Specific goals for the company, such as financial, market share, products, customers, and so on. The achievement of these specific, companywide goals will result from the achievement of specific departmental and/or team goals, which, in turn, evolve from the achievement of individual goals.

Add the fulfillment of company, departmental, and individual goals together and what do you have?

A mission accomplished.

And a vision achieved.

QUESTION

Q **"I know everything there is to know about my product, industry, and niche. What else is there to know?"**

A Suppose you've decided that the sporting goods business is the career field in which you belong. After all, you've had a sweet tooth for athletics all your life, and besides, what you don't know about sports would fit inside a downhill skier's brain. Heck, the sporting goods, er, racket should be a snap for an old jock like you.

Yeah, right.

For those of you so blissfully unaware of reality as to believe that being a sports nut leads to having a successful sporting goods business, or being a literature nut leads to having a successful bookstore business, or being a food nut leads to having a successful restaurant business, here is a mere smattering of the things, above and beyond your product, industry, and niche, that you'll have to learn your first year in business.

- How to age, and collect, receivables.
- How to age, and juggle the payment of, payables.
- How to strategize, plan, and budget for the upcoming fiscal year.
- How to maintain a perpetual inventory system.
- How to take a LIFO (or FIFO) physical inventory.
- How to understand financial statements, including balance sheets, profit and loss statements, and cash flow statements.
- How to understand the concept of cash flow, and how to manage it.
- How to grant credit and who to grant it to.

- How to (and when to) use organization charts, performance reviews, and job descriptions.
- Where to buy the right computer hardware and software, and how to use it.
- How to collect and disburse sales tax, income tax, and FICA, and how to perform all those other services the small business person is expected to perform for our needy governmental agencies.
- How to avoid discrimination suits, sexual harassment suits, and product liability suits.
- How to avoid, (and deal with when you can't) the OSHA, workers compensation, and unemployment folks.
- How to deal with drug- and alcohol-related problems, as well as smokers and nonsmokers, those of alternative lifestyles, malingerers, pilferers, and . . . .
- How to terminate an employee without getting punched in the mouth. Or shot. Or sued. Or all of the above.
- How to compute inventory turn, days-in-receivables, current ratios, and overtime pay, and how best to structure compensation plans and bonuses.
- How to (and when to) use small claims court.
- How to focus and hold people accountable and hire right and fire right and control expenses and manage a crisis and balance a culture and deal with bankers (and shareholders and vendors) and depreciate an asset and motivate employees and . . . .

Mind-boggling, wouldn't you agree? And bear in mind, this is but a mere smattering of the things you'll have to learn that first year. (I could whip up another fifty or so, given the time and inclination.)

The lesson? Knowing the way the product is made and used is important, but knowing how to manage a business is key.

Me? I'll take a sound businessperson over a master of the product any day.

QUESTION 15

Q "There are so many adverse random events (big business, the government, finding financing, interest rates, foreign competition) facing small business today. How can I hope to overcome them all?"

A Okay, so the random events you mention may be adverse, but they don't have to be fatal. In any of the situations mentioned above, the successful entrepreneur has a number of options available.

For instance:

1. *Big business.* We can move faster than they can. We can offer a degree of personal service they can't. We can get closer to the customer than they can.

   Anyway, big business should not be viewed as a competitor, but rather as a provider. It provides niches—we take advantage of them.

   And yes, big business is also a purchaser. We offer products and services, it purchases them. (We build businesses and companies, it purchases them, too.)

   In short, big business is an integral part of the capitalistic system. So are we. Long live the two of us.

2. *The government.* A major inconvenience? Yes. Necessarily fatal? No, not if we prepare for them and give them what they want and don't waste too much time complaining. (Remember, our competitors have to deal with the government, too.)

3. *Finding financing.* To the most professional entrepreneur with the best business plan go the most financing dollars.

   Financing is no random event; financing is a reward for preparation. May the best prepared entrepreneur win.

4. *Interest rates.*   Rising interest rates serve to sort out small business's wheat from its chaff. Keep your inventory and receivables under control, and you'll be the wheat.

5. *Foreign competition.*   Ditto big business.

The bottom line? The entrepreneurial profession is a profession of choices. Make more right ones than wrong ones and those adverse random events will be mere blips on your Richter Scale. Not the Big One.

PART III

Financial

How important is financing?

The quality of the financing package will either be the prelude of a successful venture or the death rattle of a doomed one.

How difficult is the search?

The search for financing is the entrepreneur's first indication of the degree of difficulty inherent in survival.

Why is financing so difficult to find?

Financing is the entrepreneur's initial test. Fail the financing question and the rest of the exam won't matter.

QUESTION 16

Q "Public or private?"

A Sorry, but you're asking the wrong guy this question. I'm as private as private can be.

My understanding of this penchant to *go public*, however, is that those entrepreneurs who do take the plunge, do so because (1) they relish the availability of all that interest-free capital, and/or (2) they relish the liquidity that comes from the public markets.

Interest-free capital? Well, it might be interest free, but it won't be for long; the cry for dividends will soon become deafening. And even if it is interest free, it sure won't be hassle free. Not by a long shot. Not when you consider all the fuss that shareholders or the Securities and Exchange Commission (SEC) or the media can make. Not when you consider the amount of the chief executive officer's time that is wasted keeping those interested parties happy and/or at bay. Not when you consider the company's cash that must be spent keeping all those outsiders out of your hair.

Liquidity? Sure, it'd be nice to be liquid for once in our loan-guaranteed life, but at what cost? Maybe when it's time to move over or move on, *going public* makes sense, but not one minute before. Public CEOs have too many distractions from running their businesses, like explaining disappointing quarterly earnings reports, mollifying dissident shareholders' concerns, or satisfying nosey media types, not to mention keeping the old price-earnings ratio afloat. No sir, not for me, all those stockholder relations chores; I've got better things to do, like training new employees, working with old customers, and developing fresh products.

Thanks, but no thanks. I'll take one banker over a few thousand shareholders anytime. I'll also take a few select inside shareholders who know what the score is to a few thousand random shareholders who don't have a clue—and don't care, as long as the dividends keep rolling in.

QUESTION 17

Q "Minority shareholders—yes or no?"

A Yes and no.

Yes, when your company absolutely, positively needs either the cash or the minority shareholders' active involvement. And an even more enthusiastic yes when you can get both cash and active involvement from the same persons.

And an impassioned yes when you make minority shareholders out of employees, whether through bonus plans, stock options, or an employee stock option plan (ESOP). After all, this move toward making owners out of employees is one that is escalating in popularity throughout the United States, and if your company isn't a part of the movement, you'll soon be left in capitalism's dust. The results are in. Now we know. Ownership begets commitment.

A warning however. When creating minority shareholders, an ironclad buy-sell agreement is an absolute must. That's because both parties need their rights defined and both parties need an exit agreement. But never make a stock offer or consummate an ownership deal without first consulting an attorney. This is one time lawyers earn their fees.

A resounding no to minority shareholders for any other reason. And a doubly resounding no to minority shareholders who are also inactive outsiders. History has proven that minority shareholders can, and most assuredly will be, a pain in certain anatomical zones given half the chance. Your reason for creating them had better be good.

I'm not saying that minority shareholders have been granted a golden bill of rights as a result of owning your company's stock. I've been on both sides of the nonpublic stock-ownership table and can relate from experience that a minority shareholder has about the same rights as a minority goldfish. Personally, I wouldn't want to be one (a minority shareholder) unless I was an integral part of the team or I could smell a one-of-a-kind opportunity that was worth sublimating my rights while keeping my mouth shut—neither of which am I good at.

QUESTION 18

Q "What are the different kinds of financing available?"

A What are you looking for? Debt or equity?
Here are the most common providers of the two:

DEBT

1. *Friends and relatives.* Most start-up businesses, especially if they are anything like mine, must first look to friends and relatives for capital. After all, this is where we've been borrowing money ever since grade school. Besides, there are no complex guarantees and no everlasting red tape where friends and relatives are concerned. It's business based on a hand shake, the best way of all.

   And so it was with me. I financed my first business with capital from friends and relatives. Some of the financing was in the form of debt, some was equity. Sure, I would have preferred a bank loan (I'd rather tell a banker than my mother or best friend that I'd lost all their money), but, as with most undercapitalized entrepreneurs, no banks would listen. Small wonder—I didn't have the necessary collateral, I didn't have the recommended experience, and I didn't know a business plan from the Marshall Plan. Thus, my only alternative, given my inexperience and naivety, was friends and relatives. Fortunately, it worked for us all.

   And so it should be for most first time entrepreneurs who aren't sure where to begin looking for start-up capital. Friends and relatives are usually the first place to stop, but you'd better be right. Nothing hurts more than to lose a friend's or a relative's money.

2. *Angels.*   If friends and relatives don't work, try angels. Angels are usually current or ex-entrepreneurs with money to spare. The good news? They've worn our shoes before and they understand how the game is played. The bad news? First, they're tough to find. Second, most angels are looking for equity while most entrepreneurs should be looking for debt. (See Question 26 for more details on angels.)

3. *Bankers.*   Debt has always been my favorite tool for capitalizing a business, and it should be yours, too, if the deal is right. That's because equity-bearing shareholders have more nitpicking rights than debt-bearing bankers and can be a lot more troublesome.

   Hey, bankers get a bad rap in the small business community. Sure, they live in their own little world and have difficulty understanding entrepreneurs and the way we operate, but it's our job to open their eyes and train them and keep them informed. In my mind, that's a small price to pay for what they can offer in return.

   And a small price to pay when compared to the things we must do to placate those equity-bearing shareholders. (For more on bankers, see Questions 21 and 22.)

4. *Microenterprise lenders.* Often government backed, these lenders specialize in small loans (up to $25,000) that banks can't profitably process. To find the microenterprise lender in your area, call the Aspen Institute in Queenstown, Maryland, at (410)820-5326, and request *The Directory of U.S. Microenterprise Programs.* Or call the SBA office nearest you.

5. *Factors.*   Factors are finance companies who advance money against our accounts receivables. In exchange for those monies, the factor then charges interest (a specified percentage over the prime rate), in addition to collecting an up-front commission fee. This early receipt of cash negates the sizeable cash requirements of carrying receivables.

   Sound too good to be true? Well, it's true all right, but brother, it's too good to be inexpensive—and it isn't. Your company's profit margins had better be deep and wide, because the expense of "being factored" is not inconsequential. Also, the factors themselves don't win any congeniality awards when dealing with those customers of yours who take longer than normal to pay. Factors should be used only as a last resort.

To find the factors who specialize in your industry, ask your industry trade association.

6. *Credit cards.*   An expensive way to borrow money, but oh so handy, for the first-time bootstrapper anyway. Besides, credit card companies don't ask questions about how the money is to be spent, they allow payments to be stretched out forever, and they don't require personal guarantees.

   I don't recommend using credit cards (because of their high interest rates), but I wouldn't be above it, if I couldn't find the money elsewhere.

7. *Your state government.*   Most state governments have an economic development program designed to help small business. What's more, believe it or not, some state programs actually have cash to loan.

   Check with your state government. Every state calls their program something different, but most of these programs are a part of the state's department of commerce.

8. *SBA financing.*   Always unpredictable, always enmeshed in red tape, and always passed on to a bank anyway. The SBA doesn't actually loan the money, it only guarantees the loan. Similar to factors, SBA loans should be considered only as a last resort. Call (800)827-5722 for the SBA office closest to you.

EQUITY

1. *Partners.*   Partners can be very difficult to deal with, but failure can be even worse. Never say no to the right opportunity with the right partner. It's a fact that partnerships outperform sole proprietorships by a wide margin. (For more on the subject of partners, see Question 10.)

2. *Venture capitalists.* Venture capitalists are individuals, or groups of people, whose primary aim is to purchase equity in growing companies and then, within a designated period of time, sell that investment at a substantial profit. This selling

process usually includes taking the company public. Most venture capitalists prefer to purchase equity in ongoing businesses (as opposed to start-ups), and generally specialize in so-called *high-tech* industries. The returns venture capitalists expect from their investments are astronomical, especially when compared to the returns the typical *low tech* small business is capable of generating.

Don't hold your breath when approaching venture capitalists. They do approximately 1 percent of the deals they see, and those that they do they insist on being closely involved in the management of the business. The streets of Silicon Valley and other exotic, high tech cities are filled with the shuffling feet of company founders who have gotten the boot as a result of a tiff with their venture capitalists. Beware, be careful, and don't waste your time with venture capitalists, unless you have the world's sexiest high tech business and would be content to tow someone else's line instead of your own.

Still interested? Call or write the National Venture Capital Association, 1655 North Fort Meyer Drive, Suite #700, Arlington, Virginia 22209 for the names of the venture capital firms in your area.

3. *Angels, friends, and relatives.*   The same angels, friends, and relatives that we discussed when talking about debt can just as well hold out for stock (equity) in lieu of debt. While most entrepreneurs would logically prefer accumulating debt to sharing equity, no two situations are the same. When in doubt as to which would work best for you, ask your accountant for advice.

See my earlier discussion on angels, friends, and relatives. Basically, the same conditions apply to equity as to debt.

4. *Going public.*   This method of raising capital is usually reserved for ongoing businesses with a long-standing track record, where the founder has a recognizable and credible name (like Steven Jobs of Apple Computer, Next, and Pixar fame) and an extraordinary small business background.

Sorry. Going public is not for most ordinary souls.

Oh yes, there is one more way to finance a business. Wait for Ed McMahon. The odds may not be as good as approaching a friend, but they're better than asking a venture capitalist.

QUESTION 19

Q "Why is financing so difficult to locate?"

A Contrary to entrepreneurial opinion, commercial bankers are not monsters or gargoyles. Neither are venture capitalists, investment bankers, or the rest of the financial community. Instead they are people, regular everyday, off-the-street, air-breathing people, just like you and me.

What's more, at least when we see them, bankers are regular everyday people doing their job, which just happens to be looking for opportunities to place their money in someone's pocket. Over the long run, if they don't locate enough borrowers, their employers won't collect enough interest and their jobs won't be justifiable. They'll soon be on the outside of those marbled foyers looking in.

See what I mean? The minute those people with money to lend (or invest) confirm an appointment with you, they are secretly hoping your proposal turns out to be a keeper. Despite our perception to the contrary, we disappoint them when it's a dud.

My advice? Get that chip off your shoulder for the financial folks—it doesn't do any good. They want us to succeed, and when our dreams don't fly, it isn't their fault. It's ours. We haven't impressed them enough.

So what impresses the keepers of the cash? What do we have to do to have our dreams taken seriously?

In order of importance, people with money to invest are looking at:

1. *Us.* First and foremost, those financial people are studying us. The entrepreneur. The boss-to-be. The asset-of-last-resort. In their eyes, anyway, if we don't pass muster, the rest of the package really doesn't matter.

This whole issue of finding money should, incidentally, be taken personally. After all, when a banker rejects our deal, he really isn't rejecting our widget; he's rejecting us. The widget could be the finest widget ever assembled, but if we aren't perceived as being able to sell it, market it, manufacture it, or direct the people who will be selling, marketing, and manufacturing it, what difference does the widget make?

Remember, at this stage of the deal, financial people aren't looking for dreamers. They're looking for doers. Doers to be led by us.

2. *Our business plan.*   More than anything else, a business plan is the entrepreneur's first order of business. It is, to outsiders, the first real indication of how the business is going to be managed. If the business plan is thorough, on target, and prepared professionally, then it is assumed by whoever is perusing it that this is the way the entrepreneur will manage his or her business. Likewise, if the business plan is hastily thrown together, error filled, and looks like yesterday's newspaper, it is assumed our business (and the investor's or lender's cash) will be managed in a similar fashion.

Though the business plan is an operational guide, its directions will change the first day it is used; thus, the contents are not all that important. After all, change is a constant in the business of small business, and it's reaction to change that counts.

Above all, the business plan is a sales tool. A sales tool directed at those people who are considering putting their money where the entrepreneur's dreams are.

They've learned from past experience . . . the better this first order of business, the more likely the second order of business will be a success.

3. *The idea.*   Is the idea important? Of course it is.

Is it a gamebreaker? No.

The lender or investor knows that, with a few exceptions, if the entrepreneur is right, it doesn't matter how unique or mundane the idea is.

Think about it. I'm sure when Steven Jobs and Bill Gates showed up for their first venture capital appointment, their listeners had to be stunned by the uniqueness of their product. Conversely, when Sam Walton showed up to sing the praises of yet another retail establishment, his listeners must have had a hard time staying awake. The unique and the mundane—both have their place.

QUESTION 20

Q "How can I find the right banker?"

A Stand on the nearest streetcorner and look for a man (or woman) you'd least like to party with.

Just kidding. (Hey, entrepreneurs get stereotyped, too.) Here's some better advice.

1. *Understand what makes bankers tick.* A bank is the most conservative of all financial resources. Their public charter is to protect their depositor's money, and when they fail all kinds of hell awaits those who are responsible. Bankers (the good ones, anyway) take this responsibility seriously. Understand going in that their conservatism is a necessary by-product of their job.

2. *Get that chip off your shoulder.* Don't be the stereotypical, tunnel-visioned, banker-hating entrepreneur; bankers are only doing their job, just like you're doing yours. Try and make their job easier instead of harder. You'll be rewarded when you do.

3. *Head in the right direction.* Banks, like other businesses, have niches in which they specialize. Look for the banks who specialize in small business. (They're there; read your local newspaper ads, ask other small business owners, or call your local Small Business Development Center (SBDC) or chamber of commerce.)

4. *Don't wait until the last minute.* Bankers don't move as quickly as entrepreneurs. Loan applications and approvals can take what seems like eons to work their way through the loan origination process. Give yourself plenty of leeway. Besides, it sends a bad signal to bankers when you wait until the last minute.

5. *Do your homework.* Find out what documentation the bank requires in advance of your first meeting. Be ready with completed

forms in hand. At the minimum, most banks will require the following:

- Personal resume;
- Business plan, including pro forma financial statements;
- Personal financial statement (statement of net worth);
- Three years of personal or business tax returns (or both).

6. *Be armed to the teeth.*   Have the world's best business plan in your briefcase. See Questions 11 and 12.

7. *Look like a CEO.*   Be dressed like someone you'd be comfortable loaning money to. Yes, appearance does make a difference to bankers. (And it should; after all, it makes a difference to customers.)

8. *Spill all the beans.*   No matter how hard you try, you can't tell a banker too much. In addition to your knock-em-dead business plan, what other information can you provide? A list of your prospective customers? A bio on your competitors? Brochures? Products? Be creative.

9. *Be honest.*   Your banker knows all too well that every business venture has its risks and downsides, as well as its rewards and upsides. What are your risks and downsides? Be honest. Your banker will be waiting to hear how you address this subject.

10. *Ask for enough money.*   The worst thing that can happen to your business is that you have to come back six months later and beg for more cash. Be sure you know, and can prove, how much money you need. Then add 10 percent for contingencies.

11. *Strive to develop a personal relationship with your banker.*   Banks have short memories, bankers don't. It isn't the bank that's important here, it's the banker. Do everything you can to make sure the two of you click. (My first banker worked for three different banks in my first ten years in business. He brought me along with him every time.)

12. *Ask all the questions, get all the facts.*   Better to find out *before* the barn door gets locked than after. Be sure to find out about the following:

- Repayment options?
- Balloon or renewal options?
- Fees, applicable interest rate, and interest rate adjustment policies?

- Period of time to close the loan?
- Personal guarantee required?
- Checking or savings account compensating balance requirements?
- What help can the bank provide in promoting your business?

Finally, remember that luck isn't the primary issue when seeking a banker's money—preparedness is.

QUESTION 21

Q "How can I keep the right banker?"

A That's an easy question to answer. Just apply the Golden Rule. You know, the Golden Rule of Banker Retention:

"Treat your banker as you'd like to be treated if you had loaned money to someone you didn't know."

Here are the details on how to follow the Golden Rule of Banker Retention.

- *Treat bankers like partners.* After all, that's what they are, because they stand to lose their investment just like you do. It isn't unusual for even the most successful of small businesses to have more banker debt than shareholder equity (I did, for ten years or more). Review your banker's annual list of loan defaults if you think they make only successful deals.

- *Understand your banker's needs.* Although bankers are interested in all the aspects of your business, they have a special admiration for hard assets, because that's their last line of insurance when all else fails. Understand this fact, don't fight it, and keep impeccable records on all hard asset items, such as receivables, inventory, equipment, and real estate.

  Remember, bankers are creditors, not shareholders. As such, they look first to your balance sheet, not to your profit and loss statement. It goes with their turf.

- *Involve bankers in key decisions.* Especially those decisions that are likely to result in a need for more cash.

- *Minimize surprises.* Bankers hate surprises, especially bad ones. Keep them informed of potential problems and don't let the bad news pile up.

- *Communicate, communicate, communicate.*   You can't tell bankers too much, but you can tell them too little. Invite them to visit your business at least once a month, give them a royal tour, and have an outline ready for every meeting. (You won't have a more important meeting that day than the one with your banker. Do it up right.)

    Most importantly, call your banker whenever the news is big, be it good or bad. Bankers want to hear it from you, not from someone else.

- *Follow up.*   Send your banker a letter after every meeting, recapping everything you've discussed. You're helping him or her do the job.

- *Treat bankers like customers.*   Like it or not, you need your banker a lot more than your banker needs you. There are many more small businesses looking for cash than there is cash looking for small businesses. Make your banker feel wanted.

Remember that bankers are like employees and customers and your kids. The better you treat them, the more likely they will be to return the favor.

QUESTION 22

Q "What interest rate can I expect to pay when I borrow money?"

A The interest rate you pay will be expressed as a percentage over prime (Prime is the rate the nation's largest banks charge their biggest, healthiest, most well-heeled customers). Thus *General Motors* can borrow their money right at prime or thereabouts (maybe less), while *Ma and Pa's Cheese and Taxidermy Co.* may have to settle for 4 percent over prime (maybe more).

The prime rate itself will vary. I've seen it bask in the low single digits, I've seen it soar to the high teens. After all, it's a function of a governmental agency, which means when you expect it to zig it is most likely to zag.

The exact number of percentage points over prime is based on the banker's perception of the risk being taken when he or she hands you the bank's cash. The riskier the loan, the higher the percentage over prime. The less risky the loan, the closer to prime.

How risky will your loan appear to your banker? He or she will look at the professionalism of your business plan, the viability of your niche, the strength of your balance sheet, the experience of your management team, and the solidarity of your loan guarantee.

You say you don't like being charged four over prime? You have the option to do something about the banker's perception. Spruce up your business plan. Shore up your anemic balance sheet. Recruit additional management strength. Add collateral to your loan guarantee.

But whatever you do, don't waste time and energy blaming the banker when he offers you a deal you can't afford to accept.

The proof is in your pudding, not his. The banker is merely the judge.

QUESTION 23

Q "Are interest rates negotiable?"

A With the exception of the amount of taxes we pay and the duration of our in-laws' stay, everything in life is negotiable. Including interest rates.

The interest rate you pay is negotiable from the day your banker first quotes it to you—the same day you agree to it. That percentage is determined by a number of variable factors: how badly you want the money, the condition of your company, the state of your industry and the economy, and so on.

As months or years pass, things happen. Situations change. And as things happen and situations change, your interest rate should change, too.

Are your earnings up? Is your balance sheet stronger? Is money more readily available? Then you deserve a lower rate. Call your banker and ask for it.

Are your earnings down? Is your balance sheet gasping for breath? Is money tight? Then you can expect a higher rate.

But don't bother calling your banker. Sit tight. He'll call you.

QUESTION 24

Q "Should I sign a personal guarantee?"

A Of course you shouldn't. Neither should you prepare a professional business plan, project your cash needs for the first year of business, or brush your teeth before your banker's appointment.

Unless, of course, you want what that banker has to offer.

OK, so I'm not suggesting you walk into a bank interview with your mortgage in your briefcase, your savings book in your pocket, and the keys to your car in your hand. Signing a personal guarantee is no small matter, and many a would-be entrepreneur has lived to regret it (I did, on more than one occasion).

And remember, when asked to sign a personal guarantee, everything is negotiable. The guarantee is no exception, but it is only one small part of the overall package. Feel free to hold out for its exclusion as long as you can.

But if I were you (and I was), and my dream depended upon it (and it did), I would sign that personal guarantee in a heartbeat (and I did—four times). Let's face it, what's the option? Watching our dream go kaput? Going back to punching a clock? Giving up more than 50 percent of our business to someone else? Those were never options for me.

Still having problems with the idea of signing a guarantee? A change in perspective might help. Try putting yourself in your banker's shoes.

After all, if you don't believe in your dream enough to risk your savings, why should he?

QUESTION 25

Q "What is an *angel?* How do I find one?"

A The word *angel* is an appropriate one. Angels are usually small business veterans, current or ex, who swoop down from the financial heavens and fund needy and worthy entrepreneurs.

Too good to be true? Maybe. Okay, so these financial angels don't exactly "swoop down from the heavens." More precisely they are "discovered by digging." Discovered by the entrepreneurs who are willing to dig the deepest to find them.

And these financial angels aren't really the kind of angels we are accustomed to thinking about when we hear the word "angels," instead, they are more like bankers who specialize in small business. These financial angels have access to cash, will deal if your story makes sense, and expect to be reimbursed for their trouble.

So what's the difference between angels and bankers?

- Angels are harder to find. They don't reside in marble foyers on downtown streetcorners, and you can't find them listed between "bankers" and "barbers" in the yellow pages.
- Most angels have been down the small business pike. Unlike bankers, they are capable of (and intent upon) delivering advice along with their cash.
- Angles are not as interested in the balance sheet as they are in the profit and loss statement. And in the entrepreneur. They rely more on gut than they do on numbers.
- Angels don't have work-out departments. They do their dirty work themselves.

- Angels aren't organized or regulated, and they don't have conventions in Las Vegas.
- Angels are versatile. Debt or equity, anything goes.

So, how do you find an angel?

With difficulty. Extreme difficulty. Angels are usually passive, low-key denizens of the underground business community and prefer to be unearthed and discovered. They know that only the most aggressive entrepreneurs will find them, and they know that aggressiveness wins in the small business game.

The best way to find angels? Network with current or veteran entrepreneurs, ask your banker (that's how I found mine), or inquire of accountants, lawyers, or business brokers. Also, some government agencies might be able to help. Try your state's department of economic development, your local SBDC, or the SBA.

This much you can count on. Of all the financial alternatives, angels are the best.

If you can find them.

QUESTION 26

Q "Balance sheets, profit and loss statements, and cash flow projections. Must I understand them all?"

A If you can ask that question, I can ask this one. Should people who play professional golf for a living know how to keep score? How about professional baseball players, or professional accountants, or Fortune 500 CEOs? As a matter of fact, how about any professional in any career? Should they know how to keep score?

If your answer to that question is yes, then I ask you, is our entrepreneurial career any less professional than the careers previously mentioned? Any less demanding? Any less risky?

And if your answer to that question is that our career field is just as professional, just as demanding, and just as risky, then you have answered your own question. Yes, you must understand how to keep score. Balance sheets, profit and loss statements, and cash flow projections are designed for this purpose.

However, as important as these reports are for scorekeeping, that is not their only function. These financial statements also serve as divining rods, tools meant to help us zero in on our strengths and weaknesses and to provide us with the feedback we need to successfully solve our problems.

THE BALANCE SHEET

The balance sheet is a snapshot of our company's financial condition on the day it is compiled, usually the last day of a month, quarter, and year. When compared to prior-period balance sheets, the current balance sheet supplies the ultimate answer to the question, "Is my company better off today than it was a year (or a month or a quarter) ago?"

The balance sheet has two sides. One consists of only assets, the other of liabilities (claims against assets) and net worth (owner's equity). As a result of the vagaries of the double entry bookkeeping system, the two sides will always be equal, hence the name *balance sheet.*

Assets include current assets (those that can be quickly converted into cash), fixed or long-term assets (real estate, plant, equipment, furniture and fixtures, and any other assets used in the business), and other assets (the ever-present miscellaneous account). On the liability side of the balance sheet can be found current liabilities (debts and obligations due within 12 months), long-term liabilities (debts and obligations due over a period exceeding 12 months), and net worth or equity (what's left after the value of the liabilities has been subtracted from the value of the assets).

The percentages and ratios derived from a balance sheet (see Question 27) can tell all kinds of tales about the current health of the business. Current ratios, quick ratios, and debt-to-equity percentages are figures that will always interest bankers and creditors.

THE PROFIT AND LOSS STATEMENT

The profit and loss statement (P&L) is a compilation of old news. It's figures are derived from past accounting periods—last month, last quarter, last year. Also known as the income statement, the P&L includes sales revenues, cost of goods sold, and all related expenses over that period of time. The result of subtracting the cost of goods sold and expenses from sales revenues? Net income—the reason we're all here.

Those entrepreneurs who enjoy crunching numbers can spend many happy hours hunched over their profit and loss statements converting line item after line item into some kind of useful percentage. For instance, such figures as ROS (Return on Sales), ROE (Return on Equity), and ROI (Return on Investment) are intended to provide the answer to the questions:

1. Is my company operating profitably? or,
2. Would I be better off buying treasury bonds?

Additionally, by expressing every cost of goods sold and expense line item as a percentage of sales, the P&L reader is able to measure the company's efficiency in converting sales dollars to profit dollars.

CASH FLOW PROJECTIONS

Profitability is nice but cash is essential. Although unprofitable businesses can continue to exist for long periods of time (i.e., Continental Airlines), those without cash must eventually close their doors. That's because cash is king in the world of business, and a company's cash flow projections measure the availability of cash into the future. By effectively projecting a company's future inflow and outflow of cash, the entrepreneur can predict trouble before it arrives, thereby dealing with cash-related problems before they become serious. Or fatal.

Cash flow projections project all future incoming cash, including cash sales, collection of receivables, sale of fixed assets, and new investments. From that figure is subtracted projected outgoing cash—payment of accounts payables, payment of notes, taxes, and other obligations, and of course, all operating expenses. The resulting figure? Projected cash flow, the amount of cash that will be available to the business during that designated period of time. An excess of incoming cash over outgoing cash assures survival. An excess of outgoing cash over incoming cash? Chapter 11 bankruptcy or worse.

This issue of understanding financial statements begs another, bigger, more important question. Why is it that most career fields have sophisticated entry-level training programs while our entrepreneurial career doesn't? Why don't we have training programs in which our newcomers are required to learn how to produce and analyze balance sheets, profit and loss statements, and cash flow projections. After all, doctors, lawyers, accountants, dental hygienists, bricklayers, welders, and yes, professional golfers and baseball players are thoroughly trained and must have some kind of an official entry-level degree before they're allowed to enter their chosen career fields.

Not so for us spur-of-the-moment entrepreneurs, however. "Gimmee a fax and a phone!" is our rallying call, and "Ready, fire, aim!" is our motto. A dream, a strong back, and an aversion to risk are the only requirements for entrance into our career field.

And yet we wonder why so many of us fail?

Maybe some day capitalism will require an entrepreneurial entrance exam. Kind of an SAT test for the small business person. Without passing it, we aspiring entrepreneurs wouldn't be allowed to risk our life's savings, our employee's careers, and so many irreplaceable years of our lives.

Until such time however, the responsibility is ours to prepare on our own for becoming an entrepreneur. Learning how to read, analyze, and utilize the information from balance sheets, P&Ls, and cash flow projections is but one of the many important preparations the entrepreneur-to-be can make.

QUESTION

Q "What are financial ratios and which are the most important?"

A Financial ratios are a collection of numbers and percentages that are derived from period-ending financial statements. Studying the meaningful ratios can indicate your business's comparative strengths and weaknesses, at the same time providing you with an indication of how to improve your business's performance. Additionally, financial ratios can provide an excellent opportunity to compare your company's performance to those of benchmark industry figures. These benchmark figures can be obtained from a variety of resources, including Dun & Bradstreet, the SBA, your industry's trade association, or the larger accounting firms.

The seven most important financial ratios are discussed next.

CURRENT RATIO

The current ratio is derived from the balance sheet by dividing current assets by current liabilities. The resulting ratio answers the question, "Does your business have sufficient assets to cover its liabilities and still have something left over?"

Obviously, the higher the ratio of current assets to current liabilities, the more liquid the business (liquidity being defined as the excess of assets-that-can-be-converted-into-cash over liabilities). While any given small business's current ratio may depend on the specific industry or the time of the year the financial statement is prepared (most businesses are cyclical), a common rule of thumb is that a current ratio of 2:1 denotes a healthy business.

The current ratio is usually the first of the ratios any liquidity-obsessed banker (which includes every banker I've ever known) looks for when perusing a financial statement. Bankers insist on liquidity, and any dips in the current ratio is sure to trigger their ultrasensitive alarm system.

QUICK RATIO

The quick ratio is the ultimate current ratio. While the current ratio includes all current assets, the quick ratio includes only cash and those current assets that can be *quickly* converted into cash (usually cash, government securities, and accounts receivable). The quick ratio answers the question, "If cash inflow stopped tomorrow, how would the business cope with its outstanding debts in the next 30 days?"

Though 2:1 is a current ratio benchmark for healthy businesses, 1:1 is an acceptable target for the quick ratio. Again, this figure may vary from industry to industry and is also highly dependent upon the time of the year.

Days in Receivables

Since accounts receivable are an integral part of any small business's collateral, the banker (or any other investor or creditor) needs to know exactly how collectable they are and how long it will take to turn them into cash. This figure (expressed in a number of days) is derived by dividing a company's annual net sales by 365, the number of days in a year. The resulting number is then divided into the current accounts receivable figure from the balance sheet. The answer represents the number of days that an average sale will remain in accounts receivable before it will be converted into cash.

The significance of days-in-receivables? A sale and the obligation that results from that sale when cash is not tendered (an account receivable) is of no help to a business until it is turned into cash. As a matter of fact, receivables require cash to fund, which means that receivables that take a long time to collect must be funded either by existing equity or by borrowing. Thus days-in-receivables is an important indicator of how well a company's cash is flowing.

Again, acceptable days-in-receivables figures will vary from industry to industry (my last business's customers included the nation's leading retailers, and they are the slowest payers on earth; thus our days-in-receivables were always high). The rule of thumb here is that a days-in-receivables of 40 or lower is acceptable while anything over 40 days means that the business's receivables are taking too long to collect, and cash is not flowing as smoothly as it should.

INVENTORY TURN

This figure answers the question, "Do I have too much cash tied up in inventory?" The number represents the frequency with which inventory *turns over* and is arrived at by dividing the cost of goods sold (from the P&L) by the year's average inventory (from the year's beginning and ending balance sheets). The higher the inventory turn, the more sales the business has in relation to its inventory. Thus an inventory turn of ten would indicate that Business #1 is actively turning its inventory ten times a year, while a turn of five for Business #2 would indicate that that business is not using its inventory as efficiently as Business #1. The bottom line? Business #2 either has too much inventory or too little sales—or both.

Acceptable inventory turns vary from industry to industry and from product to product. Grocery stores, for instance, may turn their inventory fifteen times a year, while clothing stores might be content with a turn of four times a year. Since grocery stores sell their products at very small profit margins compared to clothing stores, this disparity is acceptable.

RETURN ON SALES (ROS)

The return-on-sales percentage comes from the P&L and is determined by dividing net profit dollars by total sales dollars (revenues). The resulting percentage measures a business' ability to turn a sales dollar into a profit dollar, and can be impacted by any one of three different factors:

1. Sales volume or revenues (the more the better);
2. Expenses (the less the better);

3. Profit margin (the higher the prices on products sold the better, and the lower the costs on products purchased the better).

The rise and fall of this ratio provides an excellent barometer of how well a company is being managed and is watched carefully by those interested in the person, or persons, responsible for management. It is difficult to generalize acceptable ROSs, as they vary more than most ratios from industry to industry. A grocery business, for instance, might be ecstatic with a 4 percent ROS, while a software manufacturer would consider booting its management team after posting a 10 percent return.

RETURN ON EQUITY (ROE)

This percentage measures the efficiency with which the business is utilizing its owner's equity. It is determined by dividing net profit dollars (from the P&L) by average equity (the owner's average net worth over the preceding 12 month period). The resulting percentage measures the degree by which the owner's equity is producing income. If, for instance, the ROE is 3 percent, the owner might question whether to liquidate the business and invest its remaining equity in T-bills. (Under the assumption that T-bills are easier to manage than small businesses.) On the other hand, a return on equity of 15 percent would indicate that the owner's equity is being managed efficiently.

RETURN ON ASSETS (ROA)

The ROA percentage measures the efficiency with which the company utilizes its assets for generating income. It is determined by dividing net profit dollars by total assets.

Though ROS is usually considered a more accurate measure for judging management's performance, ROA can be important, too, especially in industries that are asset heavy, such as railroads and steel mills. On the other hand, for a manufacturer's rep business with few or no resources tied up in assets (real estate, inventory, accounts receivable), the ROA figure would be of little consequence.

PART IV

Employees

Q "What does it take to place a product on the shelves, to turn a plan into reality, and to make a dream come true?"

A Employees.

QUESTION 28

Q "What is the single most important duty the entrepreneur performs?"

A We've determined (at least I hope we have) that the entrepreneur is the single most important factor in the success or failure of his or her business. With that in mind, the question can now be rephrased to read, "What is the single most important duty the single most important individual in any small business performs?"

And the answer is:

The entrepreneur's single most important duty is to assemble a team of superstar employees in gamebreaker positions.

Once that has happened, guess what? Whatever the entrepreneur's second most important duty is can be delegated to a superstar.

Given that answer, which is the single most important lesson the entrepreneur must learn, we now must break it down into its components.

1. What are gamebreaker positions?

    Every company has between three and six gamebreaker positions. Gamebreaker positions are pivotal jobs, such as the entrepreneur (the president), the sales manager, the financial person, the marketing manager, and the operations/production manager. (See Question 38 for further information on how to identify, and fill, these gamebreaker positions.)

2. What is a superstar employee?

    The traits of a superstar employee will vary, depending on the needs of the entrepreneur and the culture of the organization. Qualities such as loyalty, creativity, a sharing of ethics and principles, and the ability to work in a crowd are characteristic of most small business superstar employees. (For further discussion on this subject, see Question 37.)

3. What does it take to assemble the team?

To most entrepreneurs, assembling a team of superstar employees is a long, drawn out, brain-dulling, not-to-be-mistaken-for-the-thrill-of-bungee-jumping process. The four components of team assembling are (1) hiring, (2) training, (3) motivating, and yes, when all else fails, (4) firing. (The specifics of each of these subjects are discussed at length in later chapters.)

Every entrepreneur, no matter where his or her strengths may lie, must spend a significant amount of time performing these four team-building activities. For instance, a small business owner with more than 25 employees should be spending at least 50 percent of his or her time assembling the team. Two hundred employees? Try 75 percent of the time. This is no part-time chore we're talking here.

The problem? These are not the kind of activities that we gunslinging entrepreneurs spend our days and nights and weekends dreaming about. What moving-and-shaking entrepreneur worth his or her bank guarantee wants to interview and re-interview, check references, train employees, write job descriptions, set goals, write performance reviews, and yes, fire nonperforming employees, when instead he or she could be meeting with customers, creating new products, and designing unique marketing plans. See what I mean? The process of team building is not entrepreneur-friendly.

But it *is* entrepreneur-necessary. And, the typical entrepreneur's complaints to the contrary, there is no excuse for his or her failure to assemble a superstar team. There are plenty of potential superstars out and about.

It's up to the entrepreneur to find them.

QUESTION 29

Q "My employees just don't get it. Is it them or is it me?"

A Sorry, it's you.
It used to be . . . .

When yesterday's entrepreneurs would hire a new employee, they'd sit back on their haunches, cross their arms, and wait for the new hire to make the grade. After all, he or she was damn lucky to have the job . . . there weren't *that* many career-type opportunities or enlightened employers around town. And even if there was, the new employee couldn't go searching for them; he or she wasn't sure where to look, and besides, job-hopping didn't look so hot on the resume. And so . . . the new hire would remain on the payroll, at least until *the entrepreneur* decided it was time for him or her to move on.

Yesterday's entrepreneur waited and watched to see how appreciative the new hire was and whether he or she produced. And then, once the employee had passed the entrepreneur's muster, only then were the floodgates of opportunity opened. Only then did the entrepreneur allocate the time and money necessary to train them, motivate them, and provide them with an environment that encourages new employees to grow and prosper.

In short, the burden of proof was on the employee to deliver. Then, once that took place, it would be the entrepreneur's turn.

No more. Today . . . .

The onus is on us, today's entrepreneur, to first provide the opportunity and environment for the employee to succeed. To accomplish this, we must train our fledgling employees, and set goals for them, and review their performance, and provide them with a long list of benefits and perks and other incentives to perform. Plus we must let them know up front what they can expect from us. We must provide an environment that encourages them to deliver.

Why? Because today's employees, the good ones anyway, have too many options. There are too many other good jobs around town, jobs that can offer qualified applicants a long list of opportunities, options, benefits, and perks. What's more, because of the proliferation of information these days, the good employees know who it is that is offering those jobs and where they can go to find them. They won't waste their time with us.

In short, the burden of proof is now on the entrepreneur. Our roles have been reversed: *First* we provide the opportunity and the environment, and *then* the new employee will deliver.

It's a mind set issue we're talking here. Once we've realized the number of options that our employees have, once we've realized we aren't the only show in town, and once we've realized the burden of proof to deliver is on us, then we will be able to attract, and keep, the kind of employees we need.

QUESTION

Q "Why can't my employees get along?"

A Because people are people, that's why, and people have this inherent need to eat, sleep, and conflict. This process began with Adam and Eve and continues with us, and the eating, sleeping, and bickering has never stopped.

Hire your first employee and what happens? You get more work accomplished at the same time you create more conflict. You can count on it.

Hire your second employee and what happens? Still more work accomplished and even more conflict created. Third employee, fourth employee, fifth employee? More work and more conflict, more work and more conflict, more work and more conflict.

The *more work* part is the result of leverage.

The *more conflict* part is the price managers of people pay for that leverage.

Thus, resolving conflict is one of the primary duties of every entrepreneur, or every manager of people. Unresolved conflict only results in more unresolved conflict, and the cost of leverage continues to rise.

I'm not saying that resolving conflict will replace a weekend at the lake on your own personal fun meter, but resolving conflict is a necessary evil of assembling a team. (Unless of course, you enjoy resolving conflict, in which case you should consider marriage counseling.) Conflict's natural tendency (like hot air), is to rise and expand, and soon all those minor unresolved spats become major unresolved conflicts, which in turn grow into all-out wars.

Here are some of the messages we leaders of people send when we don't resolve the conflicts around us:

- We don't care.
- We won't deal with problems.
- We are managerial wusses.
- We play favorites. We allow bullies to rise to the top.
- We can be manipulated by whoever it is that makes the most noise.

Now I ask you, are these the qualities of leaders?

Okay, so we've determined that resolving conflict is an important part of managing people. But how do we do it? Here are several tips:

- Don't dive into conflict, wade into it. Slowly, gingerly, carefully. Prepare for the conflict resolution process like you would any other important business deal, because that's exactly what it is—an important business deal.
- Keep personalities out of the conflict resolution process. The intent should not be to change a person's behavior, but rather to increase his or her understanding of the situation, thereby affecting change.
- Give everyone a chance to vent during the conflict resolution process.
- The key to effective conflict resolution is listening. Listening by the person doing the resolving and listening by the conflictees.
- Offer alternatives to the conflicting situation. Allow the conflictees to negotiate.
- Be a negotiator. Make compromise your goal.
- Keep the resolution confidential. Conflictees have egos, too. Protect them.
- Search for a *win-win* resolution, not a *you win* or *I win*.

It's a fact. One of the tests of becoming a successful leader of people is our willingness to face conflict.

The choice is ours. If we avoid taking the test we are sure to flunk it.

QUESTION 31

Q "Why don't my employees respond like I would if I were an employee?"

A Because your employees aren't like you. As a matter of fact, they're not even close.

According to those folks who study such things, here is a list of the typical employee's career-type motivators. The ten favorite reasons why employees show up for work in the morning:

1. Appreciation/recognition.
2. Feeling like a part of the team.
3. Getting help with personal problems.
4. Security.
5. Money.
6. Interesting work.
7. Opportunity.
8. Loyalty to company.
9. Working conditions.
10. Discipline.

Had enough? Okay, now let's take a look at the four favorite reasons (as I see them anyway) that the typical entrepreneur shows up for work in the morning (pick any one):

1. A need to achieve.
2. A desire to create.

3. A thirst for money.

4. The allure of power.

See what I mean? The two lists aren't even close. Most entrepreneurs don't give a hoot about recognition (as a matter of fact, many of us prefer to work in obscurity). And most entrepreneurs usually aren't meant to be team players; that's one of the reasons we flunked employee careers in the first place. And most entrepreneurs not only don't look for help with their personal problems, they don't look for help with any problems, personal or otherwise.

Security and entrepreneurs? Yea, sure.

And so it goes. The typical employee is a totally different animal than the typical entrepreneur. Which doesn't make either of us wrong, it only makes the two of us different.

And vive that différence, where running a business is concerned anyway. After all, imagine what our company would be like if it were populated with employees like us? Who would maintain the books day after routine day, who would make sure all those eye-rolling details were resolved, and who would take care of the grunt work that needs to be done? It wouldn't be us, that's for sure. Or anyone like us.

Besides, how many of our employees would be content to work for a wage if he or she were anything like us? Wouldn't they be constantly searching for a company of their own?

So . . . it's the entrepreneur's job to recognize these differences, and once we've recognized them, to motivate our employees not by attempting to change them, but by recognizing their needs and attempting to satisfy them—needs such as recognition, being a part of the team, and security.

After all, isn't that how the employee/employer relationship is supposed to work? You solve your employees' problems and they'll solve yours.

QUESTION 32

Q "There are so many critical issues in the day-to-day running of my business . . . from computers to receivables, from cash flow to inventory. How can I find the time to manage and lead my employees?"

A First, a touch of theory (I'll keep it short).

There are two theorems that cover everything that happens in the small business world:

> **THEOREM #1:** "No team can rise above the quality of its people."

And . . .

> **THEOREM #2:** "No people can rise above the quality of their leader."

What Theorem #1 means is that everything that happens in a small business is a function of its people. If the business is having computer problems, it is really having people problems. The computer problem is only the symptom. If the business is having cash flow problems, it is really having people problems. Cash flow is only the symptom. And if the business is having profitability problems, it is really having people problems. Profitability is only the symptom.

Think about it. A computer problem isn't a hardware problem, or a software problem, it's a people problem. Someone ordered the hardware. And someone selected the software to go with it. And someone okayed the invoice to pay for it. And someone had it installed. And if the computer isn't working properly, it's either because it was ordered incorrectly (by that someone) or it's being operated incorrectly (by another someone).

That's how Theorem #1 works. It works that way for computers and it works that way for receivables and it works that way for cash flow and inventory, too.

Now enter Theorem #2. "No team can rise above the quality of its leader." That leader is you, and your team can only be as good as your capacity to manage and lead them.

So I ask you, how can you *not* find the time to manage and lead your employees? After all (what a deal), all you have to do is manage, train, and motivate them and then leave them alone. They'll take it from there.

Q **"Do I need an employee manual?"**

A What's the first thing you do after you've purchased an appliance, computer, or automobile? You read the instructions, right? After all, you want to know how your new purchase functions and what to expect from it.

Should a new employee expect any less after buying into a new career?

Wouldn't you expect written instructions if you were a new employee? Wouldn't you want to know from the beginning exactly how your new company functions and what to expect from it? Wouldn't it make your new job easier and more employee friendly? Wouldn't a well written employee manual add a touch of professionalism to your job?

And if those reasons aren't enough, isn't it better from the vantage point of the employer, in this age of drop-of-the-hat litigation, to put your rules and regulations and expectations in writing? What's more, the process of compiling an employee manual will force you to consider policies that you otherwise might let ride . . . until it's too late.

The bottom line? The employee manual is a win-win tool, because it benefits both employer and employee.

Here are several tips on how to assemble your employee manual.

- Find a working model to use as an example. Either borrow an existing employee manual from another small business or buy one from a computer software store.
- Be sure to include an up-front disclaimer that your employee manual is not a legal document and is subject to change.

- What better place to include a statement of the company's visions, missions, and goals?
- Include an equal opportunity statement.
- Include a sexual harassment statement. Consult your attorney for the wording du jour.
- Itemize all available benefits, including health insurance, maternity leave, 401ks, profit sharing, pensions, memberships, and so on. Also include your health insurance plan as an attachment.
- Develop and describe drug and alcohol polices, including pre-employment screening and postaccident testing (if any).
- Include holiday and vacation policies.
- Define workday policies. Include issues such as working hours, overtime pay, time off, breaks, lunch hours, and designated smoking areas.
- Outline performance expectations. Include performance review policies as well as promotion and wage-increase criteria.
- Include causes for disciplinary action and termination, along with severance pay policies.
- Finally, keep the manual current. Post all changes on the bulletin board and hand out supplements when changes are made.

I'll be the first to admit that employee manuals are not exactly entrepreneurally friendly. They are time consuming to assemble, they don't visibly enhance the product or service, and they don't bring revenue to the bottom line. But they do add clarity and understanding and professionalism to the process of dealing with the company's number one asset—its employees.

QUESTION 34

Q "What are the basic components of assembling a team?"

A Assembling a team is no problem. Just haul out the check book, pay big bucks in the form of salaries, and give everyone a lifetime membership to the local country club. You'll have a team faster than you can say the word "squander."

But assembling a good team? A committed team? A team of employees who are looking for more than just a place to hang their hat?

Here are the basic components of assembling a team of committed employees.

HIRING

Committed team members won't appear on your doorstep dressed in swaddling clothes. Instead they must be located, interviewed, and finally, enticed to become a member of your team, all separate and distinct functions of the hiring process. This process, when done right, is a long and tedious procedure, yet it is the single most important team-building duty of the entrepreneur.

TRAINING

Team members, once hired, must then be trained. They must be trained to perform their individual job functions (the easy part) and they must be trained to become a contributing member of the team (the hard part). The former is a short-term assignment, the latter a long-term commitment.

MOTIVATING

Without motivation, employees show up for work because they *have to.* As in, they *have to* eat, they *have to* pay the rent, or they *have to* buy a six pack of beer.

Committed employees, on the other hand, come from the ranks of people who show up because they *want to,* as in, they *want to* be a part of the team, they *want to* do the job right, and they *want to* build a successful career. The key to making people *want to* is motivation, and motivation's tools include such aids as job descriptions, organization charts, performance reviews, compensation packages, information sharing, and employee empowerment.

FIRING

One bad hire in a key position (the proverbial rotten apple) has the potential to impair an otherwise committed team's development. Knowing how, and when, to stop the bleeding is an important part of the team-building process.

These four components will be discussed at length in following chapters. Suffice it here to say that effective team building is no accident—it is a well-thought-out, step-by-step, ongoing process that will, as a company grows, occupy more and more of the entrepreneur's time and energy.

If it doesn't, the team will suffer. Along with the entrepreneur.

QUESTION 35

Q "How can I locate and hire the best employees?"

A First, understand that the process of hiring is not exactly entrepreneur-friendly. Rather, it is a detailed, boring, inch-by-inch process, and one that cries out with the need for follow-up, listening, and attention to detail. Not exactly the way most entrepreneurs prefer to spend their time.

But hiring must be recognized for what it is: the entrepreneur's most important day-to-day duty. How else can a team of superstars be assembled? How else can a company of committed employees be found?

So . . . hiring should be placed on the top of the entrepreneur's to-do list, and there it must remain until the hiring has been successfully completed. Effective hiring is so important it is the one job the entrepreneur should never delegate.

Hiring isn't that important, you say? Then try attaching a cost to its failure. Try determining what it will cost to hire the wrong person? The cost will equal the expense of the mistakes that are sure to follow plus the cost of wasted training time plus the time and energy required to kick start the process all over again.

Incidentally, an endless list of benefits results from hiring correctly. The development of a team filled with superstars leads the list, followed closely by the fact that the better the employee, the less time must be spent managing him or her. The result? More free time to pursue whatever the entrepreneur wants to pursue.

And don't tell me there aren't a lot of good candidates available. Potentially good employees abound, and to the entrepreneur who is willing to go to the most trouble to find them will go the employee spoils.

Here is a list of hard-earned tips on the subject of hiring.

1. Never interview a candidate without first preparing a written job description (see Question 43). The good interviewees will want to know exactly what the job entails.

2. Involve other key employees in the hiring process, (i.e., employees who have a stake in the success or failure of the job). Then compare notes, remembering that yours is not the only discerning eye in town.

3. Look close to home first, and when in doubt, hire the insider. Insiders require less training, and their promotion sends the right message to the rest of the team.

4. Remember, the job you are offering isn't the only opportunity in town. If the candidate is a potential superstar, he or she will have other options in addition to yours. Be ready to assume the role of seller in the hiring process.

5. The interviewing process is an extended meeting over an extended period of time. Prepare for it as you would any other important meeting. Have an agenda, a time frame, and include handouts where necessary.

6. The stronger the candidate, the more difficult he or she will be to sign. The negotiation process may be rough and turbulent, but hold your temper, and understand what's going on here. The two of you aren't conflicting, you're negotiating—a key ingredient in the team-assembling process. Besides, wouldn't you prefer to have a tough negotiator on your team?

7. Don't trust the candidate's references, they are usually friends. Find references of your own using the candidate's past job connections, past customers, or your own internal networks. Take notes during the course of the interview and look for clues to these nonresume references.

8. The candidate will be both talking and listening during the course of the interview (hopefully more of the former than the latter). Take note of his or her capacity to do both, remembering that if the interviewee can't listen, he or she won't be able to work in a crowd. (You're hiring a team member here, not an individual performer.)

9. Look for a match in such cultural issues as ethics, principles, and values, especially when hiring staff employees. Cultural

mismatches are deeply ingrained and always difficult to over-come in the team-building process.

10. Listen carefully, then dissect the applicant's questions. Can you tell from the questions what's important to him or her? Can you tell what isn't? Are these sensible questions or busy-work questions? In other words, how well the candidate prepares for the interview is an indication of how badly he or she wants the job.

11. Be cautious of ex-government or ex-Fortune 500 employees. They are accustomed to working in an environment light years from that of small businesses. Office politics, resistance to change, and dealing with hierarchies and "lowarchies" are a part of their cultural background. Adaption to the small business environment won't come easily for these folks.

And finally, remember that hiring's no art, it's a science, and, like any other science, it requires time and repetition to do it right. Don't dabble with the process, dive into it.

The quality of your team is at stake.

QUESTION 36

Q "What should I look for when hiring salespeople?"

A Make no mistake about it, the hiring of salespeople is far different than the hiring of administrative or operations employees. Salespeople are the quarterbacks of the small business team and the sole representative of the company to its customers. Which makes the salesperson a breed of his or her own.

Which also makes the hiring process a breed of its own.

The best sales hire I every made (we'll call her Marie) illustrates the process and the hoped-for results. Marie had answered a newspaper ad for a telemarketing position. The position entailed selling sportswear products to distributors over the telephone.

Marie appeared for our interview dressed in the latest Ralph Lauren suit. She answered my questions crisply and cleanly, her eyes never wavering from mine. She responded to my what-do-you-want-from-this-job question with a matter-of-fact answer. "I want to make money. Lots of it." When it was her turn to ask questions, she asked the right ones (she had researched us thoroughly in advance of the interview) and listened to my responses intently, taking notes. And finally, when it came time to negotiate, Marie gritted her teeth and held out for health insurance, although it wasn't a part of our beginning commissioned-salesperson's package at that time.

She got her health insurance, along with the job. And I got the best salesperson I ever hired, over a 22-year span of hiring salespeople. (Five years later she sold $5 million in sportswear products to the nation's top department stores, including such upscalers as Bloomingdales, Filenes, and Marshall Fields.)

Here's why Marie was the perfect hire:

1. *She asked the right questions. And then listened.*

     Twenty years ago the best salespeople were song-and-dance artists. The better they sang and the better they danced, the better their chance to make the sale.

     Today the game has changed. No more is writing the order or inking the customer the bottom-line purpose of the sales call. Today it is establishing a relationship.

     The first order of establishing that relationship? Solving the customer's problems . . . which won't happen unless the salesperson can determine exactly what those problems are. Which won't happen unless the salesperson is capable of asking the right questions and following up with acute listening skills.

2. *Marie was self motivated.* (In this case, by money.)

     People that need a heavy dose of motivating won't make great salespeople. (They might make great accountants or shipping and receiving clerks but they won't make great salespeople.) Marie knew what she wanted and what she must do to get it.

     I knew from that interview I wouldn't have to spend much time motivating Marie. She'd provide that part of the management formula herself.

3. *Marie's demeanor and appearance exuded professionalism.*

     The salesperson represents the company to the outside world, often to the exclusion of everyone else. My company's customers wouldn't have known our CEO, President, or CFO, from the Xerox repairman, but they certainly knew our salespeople. And they judged our company accordingly.

     Like it or not, customers do judge books by their covers.

4. *Marie did her homework.*

     Preparation is the salesperson's number one selling tool. Marie came to our interview prepared, an indication that she would use the same degree of preparation when calling on her customers.

5. *Marie had fire in her eyes.*

     Above all, I hired the fire in Marie's eyes. This *fire in the eyes* is a prerequisite of sales hiring because salespeople are the quarterbacks, the movers and shakers, and the rockers and rollers of the small business team.

QUESTION

Q "What is a *superstar* employee?"

A A *superstar* is an employee that every growing small business must have in its *gamebreaker* positions. (See Chapter 38 for specifications on gamebreaker positions.)

The qualities required of superstars depend on the entrepreneur's strengths and weaknesses, as well as the culture that he or she has created. Every small business is different.

My superstar must:

- *Share my ethics and principles.* I'm not saying my ethics and principles are right for the rest of the world. But I am saying that to be compatible and work side-by-side with me, my key employees had better share my ethics and principles.

  It's my company and there are some things I intend to dictate. Ethics and principles are two of them.

- *Grow with the company.* It's one thing to be a superstar today, it's another to be capable of becoming one tomorrow. Companies grow and companies change, superstars must be capable of growing and changing, too.

- *Be able to work in a crowd.* Individual talent is no longer enough. The emergence of teams requires that superstars be able to communicate and synergize with the rest of the team. Loners need not apply for my superstar positions.

- *Subscribe to my vision.* My superstars don't have to do things my way (in many cases we'd have been better off if they hadn't), but they do have to be heading in the same direction. My vision (for the company anyway) must be their vision.

- *Welcome change.*   Change is a constant in most small business environments, and mine is no exception.
- *Be creative.*   "This has always been the way we do things around here" won't fly in most growing small businesses. The way we do things around here is the way that works best on any given day.
- *Speaks his or her mind.*   Ideas are nothing more than ideas until they've been shared. My superstars must be willing to speak up.

Such are my qualifications for a superstar employee.
And yours?

QUESTION 38

Q "What are my company's gamebreaker positions?"

A Gamebreaker positions are those sensitive jobs that absolutely, positively must be filled by superstars before a company can prosper.

Every small business has somewhere between three and six gamebreaker positions. They are (not necessarily in order of importance, with the exception of the first): CEO (president), CFO (controller, bookkeeper), sales manager, operations manager (office manager), marketing manager (art director, creative director), and purchasing director.

Try the following exercise with your own small business.

1. Identify your gamebreaker positions.
2. List your criteria for a superstar. (See Question 36.)
3. Answer the following question: "How many of my company's gamebreaker positions are presently occupied by superstars?"
4. Where your gamebreaker positions are not presently occupied by superstars, ask yourself why. Is it because the employee in that position (a) hasn't had the necessary training, (b) hasn't been properly motivated, or (c) doesn't have the potential to become a superstar?
5. Devise a game plan to do something about (a), (b), or (c) above. For instance: (a) where training is lacking, develop a training program specifically for each gamebreaker position and enroll your nonachieving employee in it, (b) where motivation is lacking, fill in the missing motivational pieces for each superstar position (goal setting, job descriptions, performance reviews,

compensation programs, and so on), or (c) where the potential is lacking, begin the search for a successor.

Given the proper training and motivation, there is no reason why every small business should not have a team of superstars in its gamebreaker positions. After all, there are plenty of viable candidates on the streets. The only roadblock to finding them is the entrepreneur who prefers to spend his or her time doing something else.

QUESTION 39

Q **"How can I afford the time and money to train my employees when most of them won't be around that long?"**

A As someone once said, "If you think training employees and watching them leave is expensive, try not training them and watching them stay."

Ah, training—the most entrepreneurially malaigned small business employee development aid of them all. Why, it's almost as if we entrepreneurs are allergic to training; at the snap of the finger we can spout a half-dozen reasons why not to. Training, we are quick to point out:

1. Takes too much time away from the job.
2. Is too expensive.
3. Is too difficult to judge its impact on the bottom line.
4. Is a waste of resources. Most employees don't stay around long enough to justify it.
5. Is difficult to determine the results.
6. Anyway (growl, grump), the employee belongs right here. At the desk. On the job.

Sound familiar?

As a result of our in-bred allergy, training is one area where our Fortune 500 cousins hand us small business folks our lunch. They have long since recognized the need for extensive training so they extensively train their employees. Then they train them some more. Sure, it helps that they can cough up the cash to pay for all that training, but I ask you—how were they able to accumulate the cash in the first place?

That's right. By utilizing trained employees.

So, where can we small business owners, and our employees, find the training we need?

- *Schools.*   Every small business should offer a tuition-reimburse-ment program to its employees.
- *Consultants.*   Sure, they're expensive, but the right consultant is worth his or her weight in pentium chips. Network carefully to find the right one. (See Question 72.)
- *Inside your industry.*   Many vendors offer training programs on their products and on related procedures. Don't be afraid to ask.
- *Seminars.*   What are Saturday mornings for, anyway?
- *Books.*   Is one great idea worth $20 and two hours of your, or your employee's, time?

There are two kinds of training the small business must offer; on-the-job training and team training.

On-the-job training is the easiest to justify. On-the-job training begins the employee's first day on the job and is designed to help him or her assimilate the job skills necessary to perform the job. The results of on-the-job training are immediate and pleasurable, and as the em-ployee's output goes up, so does the entrepreneur's mood.

Not so with team training. Team training is the instruction of employees on how to grow and contribute to the team, and it encom-passes a wide variety of subjects, none of which are designed to imme-diately increase output. (As a matter of fact, the time taken to team train an employee decreases his or her output . . . in the short-term, anyway.) Team training comes in such soft and non-revenue-producing subjects as understanding human behavior, decision making, problem solving, conflict resolving, understanding financial statements, and grasping the importance of quality, service, and customer responsive-ness. Thus, team training is a long-term, low-immediate-impact train-ing tool, and long-term and low-immediate-impact training tools are not on the entrepreneur's list of favorite ways to spend money.

But team training should be a favorite way to spend the entre-preneur's money because it is one of the leading foes of one of our deadliest enemies.

Trial and error.

QUESTION 40

Q "Why do I have to motivate my employees? How do I go about it?"

A Everyone needs to be motivated, even entrepreneurs. The difference is that the typical entrepreneur's motivation comes from within (i.e., the internal drive for growth, power, or money), while the typical employee is not so internally inclined. His or her motivation must come from without.

Enter the entrepreneur-turned-motivator.

There are a number of motivational tools available, all of which are necessary for small business's survival and all of which are entrepreneurially unfriendly. But to the entrepreneur who is willing to spend the most time and money motivating his or her employees will go the most committed team.

Those motivational tools include:

1. *The organization chart.* Employees need to know where they stand today and where they can potentially stand tomorrow if they chose to expend the effort.
2. *Job descriptions.* Employees need to know what is expected of them.
3. *Goal setting.* Employees need defined goals to pursue.
4. *Accountability.* Employees must be held accountable to achieve those goals.
5. *Performance reviews.* Employees need feedback on their ongoing performance.
6. *Compensation plans.* Employees need to be compensated. Compensation plans should be designed to motivate as well as to reward.

7. *Positive reinforcement.*   Employees must be publicly appreciated and recognized when their performance deserves it.

8. *Negative reinforcement.*   Sometimes the bleeding must stop.

Think about it. If our machinery squeaks, we oil it.
Should we do anything less for our employees?

QUESTION 41

Q "Do I need an organization chart?"

A Wouldn't it be a relief if there was no such thing as organization charts? If we could wave our magic wand and, poof, the job would get done by the best person available to do it? How sweet it would be—just think—no politics, no hierarchies, no passing the buck.

Well don't hold your breath. The organization chart, in one form or another, is here to stay, throughout my lifetime anyway. Like it or not, organization charts are an integral part of any organization. Every team needs a chain of command . . . somebody to manage and judge performance, somebody to promote and demote team members, somebody to encourage and empower the team.

Yes, everyone must work for someone, answer to someone, and be accountable to someone. Teams, as we know them today anyway, are unable to function otherwise.

But organization charts should be molded from rubber, not cast in steel. They should be constructed to bend and to stretch, according to need and according to the people they are intended to organize. This means that the best person available to do the job should do the job, no matter what the organization chart says.

Here are several tips on how to construct and use your organization chart.

- Flatter (fewer tiers) is better when the employees are right. The stronger the team members, the fewer the management layers.
- Don't live or die by your organization chart. Use it administratively but not religiously. Flexibility is the key.
- Organization charts should be constructed to fit your employees, not vice versa. It's okay to assign responsibilities outside

the chart. Employees should be able to go where they're needed the most without being restricted by placement. In other words, dotted lines are okay.

- Don't pay by the organization chart; pay by the quality of the work and the employee's contribution to the team.

- Don't get hung up on titles. A crusade for a title sends a negative message and detracts from the team. Beware of those employees to whom titles are important.

- How many employees can one person supervise? That depends on the quality of the employees and the person doing the supervising. One would be plenty if that one were like some I've had over the years. Fifteen would be a snap if those fifteen were my best. It depends on the players.

- The number one enemy of an efficient organization chart is an inefficient management team. (And guess who is at the top of that team?)

There are as many variations of organization charts as there are companies that use them. Some charts are loosely constructed, others are tightly fitted. Some are right side up, others are upside down. Some have dotted lines, some don't.

Whatever form it's in, every organization chart should provide (1) an orderly way to solve problems, (2) an orderly way to make decisions, and (3) an orderly way to get the job done.

You say you don't like organization charts? Okay, then assemble the world's greatest team. Then train that team, motivate it, and stand back and stay out of its way.

QUESTION 42

Q "What is accountability? How important is it to my business?"

A "The buck stops here," Harry Truman would snap to anyone willing to listen, as he accepted responsibility for his latest presidential decision. Or "If you can't stand the heat, get out of the kitchen" was another oft-quoted Trumanism relating to accepting responsibility.

This act of accepting responsibility, Truman was saying, goes hand in hand with running the country or, for that matter, with running any organization. Either accept that responsibility or give up the job.

Accountability is the act of accepting responsibility and is as much a factor in the success of a small business as it is in the success of the U.S. presidency. But the buck mustn't just stop at the president's (or the entrepreneur's) desk. The buck must stop everywhere.

Answer the following questions relating to the role of accountability in your organization.

- Do you set goals and have performance standards for your employees, departments, and teams?
- Are your employees' responsibilities to achieve their goals and meet their performance standards spelled out clearly?
- Do your employees acknowledge their goals and performance standards and accept the need to be held accountable for them? Do they understand why accountability is an important element in the success or failure of your business?
- Do you follow up the accountability process? Do you reward the achievers? Do you punish the nonachievers? Is the follow-up done on a timely basis?

In other words, does your company have a culture that promotes accountability? If the answer to any of the above questions is no, then an important piece of the accountability puzzle is missing.

Here are the four pieces of that accountability puzzle. The four elements necessary to establish an accountability culture in any small business are:

1. *Defined responsibilities.*   Defined responsibilities come from the establishment of formal *performance expectations* (job descriptions) for every employee. Performance expectations outline exactly what is expected of each position within the company.
2. *Goals.*   Every employee must have on-the-job goals for himself or herself . . . goals that are established, and agreed upon, by both employee and supervisor. Every department and team must have goals, too.
3. *Feedback.*   Employees should have intermittent and timely discussions with their supervisor on the status of their progress in meeting their performance expectations and in achieving their goals.
4. *Follow-up.* Performance expectations fulfilled and goals achieved must be followed up by appreciation, recognition, and where applicable, rewards. And yes, nonachievement of performance expectations and goals must be followed up, too.

These are the four elements necessary to create and maintain a culture of accountability in any company. The need to communicate expectations and follow up, incidentally, should be nothing new to many of us; those of us who are parents have been doing it for years.

QUESTION 43

Q "Are job descriptions necessary?"

A Are clearly defined instructions necessary? How about agreed upon duties—are they necessary? And expectations of performance—are they necessary?

If your answers to these questions are yes, then job descriptions are necessary, too.

I'll admit that the term *job descriptions* sounds terribly, uh, stiff and formal, even to the extent of being Fortune 500ish. So let's change the term to something that sounds more entrepreneur-friendly. To something that goes beyond defining the job and, instead, defines the purpose of the job. Lets call that something . . .

Performance expectations.

Performance expectations . . . a modern-day descendant of yesterday's outmoded, Model-T job description. The intent of the performance expectation, in keeping with the expanded empowerment of today's employees, should not be to constrict those employees within their particular job, but rather to allow them to adapt their talents to it. Thus we don't want to limit their journey by defining the route, we only want to identify the destination.

The performance expectation is the first of a four-step employee appraisal process, a process intended to provide both employee and employer with a flexible but reliable framework for defining and measuring performance. This four-step process includes:

> **Step One:** *Performance expectations.* Defines the employer's expectations of that position and provides a reference point for determining achievement.

Step Two: *Goal setting.*   A mutual agreement between employee and employer on the expected output of that performance (see Question 44).

Step Three: *Ongoing feedback.*   Continual communications between employee and employer, intended to provide day-to-day appraisal of job performance along with progress toward achieving goals.

Step Four: *Performance review.*   A formal review of the employee's performance for the prior accountability period (usually one year). The performance review compares actual performance to expectations and evaluates achievement of goals (see Question 45).

Here are a collection of tips on how to write a performance expectation:

1. Give the position a title, if for no other reason than employees like titles.
2. Include a why, how, where, and who statement—why the job is necessary, how it relates to the mission, where it is located on the organization chart, and who are its supervisors and supervisees.
3. Define the evaluation process. Include the formal dates of the performance review, the time periods for performance review follow-up, and the channels for ongoing feedback.
4. In a brief descriptive statement, concentrate on the position's output, not on its activity. Define what is expected of that position rather than how it is expected to be performed. Don't limit the employee's creativity in performing the job. Remember, performance expectations are meant to expand jobs, not to constrict them.
5. Be flexible. Times change. So do jobs. Performance expectations should not be written in indelible ink.

Okay, so I'll agree that the anticipation of writing performance expectations does not exactly send shivers of anticipation up the typical entrepreneur's spine. But it is a one-time-duty that is an absolutely, positively necessary element of the employee appraisal process and one that will repay the preparer's misery many times over. Why? Because performance expectations provide an element of structure that is often missing in the free-wheeling entrepreneur's small business.

And, contrary to popular entrepreneurial opinion, structure is not the small business person's natural enemy. To the contrary, when used flexibly, structure can be our friend.

QUESTION 44

Q "Do my employees need goals? How do I set them?"

A Goals, as a tool for self-improvement, seem almost too good to be true. Goals simultaneously provide direction, motivation, and measurement for those of us who set them and strive to achieve them. With so many associated benefits, how can we choose not to set goals?

The answer?

We can't.

Everyone needs goals, and not just in the workplace. We need them in the raising of kids, the maximizing of relationships, and in the improvement of whatever else we set our mind to improve. And we're not talking New Year's resolutions here—we're talking goals. As in, commitments to objectives.

I'll admit that the establishment of goals puts pressure on those who establish them in a world where there's enough pressure already. Pressure to achieve, pressure to deliver, pressure not to disappoint. But goals are what give us purpose in the jobs we do.

Here's an acronym to help us set goals . . . for ourselves and for our employees. Call them our SMART goals.

S: *Specific.* Goals must be clear, direct, and definable.

M: *Measurable and meaningful.* Goals must be measurable so that supervisor and employee can assess whether or not the goals are achieved. Also, goals must be meaningful to both parties.

A: *Appropriate.* Goals should be appropriate to the employee's age, experience, potential, and responsibility.

R: *Realistic.*   Goals should be challenging but achievable. Eighty percent of the goals should be obvious, 20 percent should be a stretch.

T: *Time Limit.*   Goals should be achievable within the framework of the performance review (usually one year) and established with an eye toward creating a sense of urgency in the goal-setter's work habits.

And how should we determine our employee's specific goals? Not by dictation, that's for sure, but rather by the two of us working together to develop those goals. Developing them by using and personalizing the SMART goal-setting routine.

Here are several additional suggestions on how to set goals.

- Always put goals in writing. This formalizes the goal-setting procedure and cements the commitment.
- Never set a goal without first devising a plan on how to achieve it.
- Don't wait until the end of the goal-setting period to review progress. Do it often and informally.
- The follow-up process is as important as the goal-setting process. Follow up your employee's goals diligently and often.
- The primary reward for the *entrepreneur* achieving his or her goals should be self-satisfaction. The primary reward for an *employee's* achieving his or her goals should be recognition, and can include both financial renumeration and public announcement.
- It's okay to change goals in midstream if the reasons are right.
- It's okay if, from time to time, goals are not achieved. But nonachievement should be nonrecurring and infrequent, and there must be consequences when goals go consistently unachieved.

Goal setting in a small business environment is like everything else in this age of the empowered and enlightened employee. It is a process that should be viewed as an opportunity for both entrepreneur and employee to improve.

Then when one party benefits, the other will, too.

QUESTION 45

Q "Are annual performance reviews really necessary?"

A If this was a perfect world, we wouldn't need annual performance reviews. Instead we would communicate with our employees daily, patting them on the back when they deserved it, spanking them on the kiester when they didn't. There would be no secrets or surprises when performance review time came around. Everything that needed to be said would have been said.

This isn't a perfect world. Our employees are not perfect employees, and we entrepreneurs come up a little short in the managerial category as well. And the more imperfect the two of us are, the more we need the annual performance review.

The annual performance review is the final and complete piece of the employee motivational puzzle. It culminates the preceding year's employee appraisal process, as well as providing the occasion for the kickoff of a new year. The review is the employee's own private annual awards ceremony. (Remember the importance of recognition? Well, the boss's assessment is at the top of the recognition curve.)

The performance review should not be treated lightly. It is the culminating event of managing small business's number one asset—the employee.

The annual performance review should be held once a year, either shortly after the end of the fiscal year (to get the new year started on the right foot), or on the employee's anniversary date. In addition to reviewing the employee's past year's performance, the performance review should agree upon a new set of goals for the upcoming year as well as establishing whatever base salary and bonus options are applicable.

Finally, while the performance review is intended to serve the aforementioned multitude of purposes, there is one overriding purpose that sublimates the rest. *The performance review, first and foremost, is a tool designed to improve performance.* Not to judge performance, mind you, but to improve it. Not to change behavior, but to improve performance. Everything that happens in the course of the performance review is a means to this end.

Here are a collection of tips on how to use and improve the annual performance review.

1. There are a wide range of performance review forms and formats available, beginning with generic, fill-in-the-blank forms and ending with creative, devise-your-own formats. The generic forms are quicker and easier, but lack the personal touch. Be creative and be personal.

2. The review should not be approached as a time to dump and unload. If the reviewer has accumulated a long list of the employee's mistakes and transgressions over the reviewing period, the day-to-day managerial job isn't being done. Feedback and communication must be done on a daily, not a yearly, basis.

    The need for feedback and communication cannot be replaced by the annual performance review. It can only be abetted.

3. The more input the employee has had in creating his or her goals, the less explosive the review has the potential to become.

4. Schedule the review well in advance, giving the employee plenty of time to prepare (yes, the employee should be allowed an agenda as well).

5. The reviewer should prepare for the review thoroughly, always remembering that the review is the employee's most important meeting of the year. Bring necessary handouts, document examples of performance (both good and bad), and present a carefully thought-out, professionally prepared review. And don't forget to provide the employee a copy.

6. No secondhand data allowed. No third party comments. No useless adjectives. Be specific.

7. Document and measure. Document examples used, measure progress and/or regress.

8. Allow no interruptions during the review. Interruptions send a message of secondary importance.

9. Stress from the outset that the purpose of the review is to improve the employee's performance. Reinforce this intent throughout, especially when discussing shortcomings, deficiencies, and areas needing improvement.

10. Get the review off on the right foot. Begin with compliments and achievements. Remember, recognition and positive reinforcement improve performance, too.

11. Be honest. Sugar coating may avoid conflict but it won't resolve problems. Reviews lose their meaning when they lose their truthfulness.

    The reviewer's ultimate goal? To become known as a tough, but fair, reviewer.

12. Like everything else of importance in managing people, the review must be followed up. And followed up. The more employee improvement required, the more follow-up necessary. Formal follow-up should be monthly in extreme cases, quarterly in most cases, and always semi-annually, even for the performing superstars.

In the right hands, the performance review can be a catalyst to improving performance, and has unlimited managerial potential. In the wrong hands, the review can be an explosive and dangerous event, an occasion viewed with trepidation by both reviewer and reviewee.

Give the annual performance review the respect and attention it deserves. Approach it with only one purpose in mind—to improve the employee's performance.

Q "How important is compensation? What is the best compensation plan?"

A Remember what the experts who study motivation said about compensation? It's fifth on the list of employee motivators, they told us, the insinuation being that compensation, while important, is not the gamebreaking issue.

Yea, right. The next time annual salary time comes around, try saying no to a few expected (and deserved) raises. Or try cutting a few salaries just for fun. Go ahead, I dare you. You'll see. Fifth suddenly becomes first.

Nothing is more important than compensation on *that* particular day. That's because compensation is a black-and-white issue; employees can look at it, compare it, and take it home to their spouses. Compensation states in very real terms exactly what that particular employee is worth in the eyes of the employer. Oh yes, and compensation can also be the #1 foot-in-the-door when competitors come snooping around to hire away your best employees.

There are a number of ways to compensate employees.

- *Hourly.* Try telling McDonalds that hourly compensation (paying for time) is outmoded and doesn't work. It works for them and a lot of other employers who use part-time and entry-level employees to get the job done.
- *Annual Salary.* A long-term version of paying for time. Usually comes with annual cost-of-living raises and bonuses up to 25% of base salary (bonuses based on performance-to-plan and/or achievement of goals). Annual salary denotes security, and oh how those employees do love that security.

- *Commission.*   Always the best for the hungry, hard-charging sales types.
- *Pay-for-performance.*   (Also called gain sharing or success sharing.) An increasingly popular alternative to paying for time. Usually involves a small base salary, often without annual cost-of-living adjustments, with all other compensation based on either individual or team performance or a combination of both. Specific pay-for-performance plans are as varied and creative as small business itself, and require an efficient measuring system to back them up. But the results can be astounding.
- *Hybrids.*   A mix of annual salary, pay-for-performance, annual bonuses, stock option plans, ESOPs, and whatever else the creative entrepreneur can devise. The more creative the options and the more suited to the individual, the better the plan.

Which of the above is best for you? That depends on the employee, the position he or she has been hired to fill, and the industry you're in. Most growing small businesses can use a smattering of these options.

Several additional points on the subject of compensation:

- Make sure your employees thoroughly understand whatever formula you use to compensate them. Paying on the basis of such financial results as ROA (Return on Assets) or ROS (Return on Sales) makes all kinds of economic sense, but only if the employee thoroughly understands the concept behind the formula and how he or she can impact the results.
- Make sure you can measure whatever it is that needs measuring before you agree to pay for it. Measurement is always easier said than done.
- Be consistent within employee groups. Pay your sales people one way, your accounting types another, and your executive types another.
- Be sure your executive bonus plans allow for overall company profitability before any individual bonuses kick in. The team always comes first.
- Keep the periods of time between bonus payments as short as possible. Rewards, financial and otherwise, lose their motivational impact when stretched out too long.

- Consider an ESOP—a great way to compensate employees, and always the ultimate measure of team performance.

Finally, remember that when devising a compensation plan for your employees, you are not creating an expense account in the process, but rather developing a tool with which to motivate.

The bottom line?

No matter how much money you spend on your compensation plan, if the dollars don't motivate your employees, the plan is no good.

QUESTION 47

Q "What's the big deal about positive reinforcement?"

A Remember when you were a little kid and the lawn needed mowing? Your mom said she'd give you an ice cream cone if you mowed it and your dad said he'd give you a spanking if you didn't. Which worked best?

Well, so it is in our adult life and our family life and our small business life, too. We attract bees with honey.

Besides the logic and effectiveness behind positive reinforcement, guess what? It's also easier, requires less energy, and is a lot more fun. Heck, a pat on the back, a smile, and a "job well done" (positive reinforcement in its purest form) can be downright medicinal in its effects on the person doing it. Compare that to criticism and finger pointing and anger which can be downright tiring, unhealthy, and stressful. Besides, it doesn't work.

Remember the employee's top ten motivational list? The ten favorite reasons why employees show up for work in the morning? (See Question 31.) Well appreciation/recognition was numero uno on that list, above pay, security, and everything else.

Here is a collection of tips on how to get the most out of appreciation and recognition.

1. Actively seek opportunities to appreciate and recognize employees. (Most entrepreneurs inherently do just the opposite, that is, they actively seek opportunities to correct and criticize.) Make *appreciation quotas* every day, and don't leave the office until they've been filled.

2. Broadcast good news. Any good news. Sure, employees like to be personally recognized, but they like to be publicly recognized

even more. Make the announcement loud and clear and as wide-spread as you can.

3. Everyplace is the right place to recognize good work. On the production line, in your office or in the employee's, beside the water cooler, after work in the parking lot, over a beer. Hold official appreciation meetings for the really meaty stuff.

4. Appreciate and recognize immediately. The closer to the actual deed, the more effective the appreciation. Similar to overdue rewards, overdue appreciation loses its motivational impact.

5. Don't play favorites, spread appreciation around. The leverage may be in the sales department, but marketing folks like, and deserve, appreciation, too. So do the folks on the production line, on the shipping dock, and in the accounting office. This is a team you're appreciating here, and good teams don't play favorites.

6. Positive reinforcement shouldn't just come from the top; everyone should be involved in the process. Strive to make appreciation a part of your culture.

And remember, though we entrepreneurs may think that appreciation and recognition is no big deal, our employees aren't like us. Studies show that most entrepreneurs are intraverts and that outward displays of public appreciation embarrass us. But 70 percent of our employees are extraverts (the same studies show), and my, how those extraverts do love appreciation and recognition.

So what are you waiting for? Go ahead, pour it on.

QUESTION 48

Q "What is empowerment?"

A Empowerment is the delegation of authority and responsibility. In the case of small business, empowerment flows *down* . . . as in, down the organization chart. Down to the people who are responsible for getting the work done.

With that definition in mind, follow if you will, this question and answer thought process:

- What is a supervisor? (Answer: A supervisor is a person who manages workers.)
- What is a worker? (Answer: A worker is a person who gets the job done.)
- What does a supervisor do? (Answer: A supervisor tells workers when and how to get the job done.)
- Why do workers have to be told when and how to get the job done? (Answer: Because they haven't been properly empowered to do it themselves.)
- If workers were properly empowered, what would happen to supervisors? (Answer: They would become workers. Then they too could get the job done.)

These questions and answers point out the two advantages of empowerment to the empowerer (the entrepreneur): (1) The expense of the middleman is removed, and (2) the decision-making process is delegated to the place where it belongs—the job site.

Here are a collection of tips on how to effectively empower employees.

- The goal of empowerment should be that each employee be allowed the opportunity to reach his or her fullest potential.
- Be patient when implementing empowerment. The empowerment process is an expensive and time-consuming start-up. It won't happen overnight and it won't happen without plenty of early setbacks.
- Empowerment only works when the right employees are in place. Effective hiring must come first.
- Proper training and motivating must come next. Only when trained employees are motivated to perform is empowerment sure to follow. Empowering untrained and unmotivated employees is dangerous business.
- Effective empowerment requires the right culture in which to prosper. The right culture must:
  1. Hold people accountable.
  2. Allow mistakes.
  3. Welcome change.
  4. Encourage new ideas and participation.
  5. Allow delegation.
  6. Be flexible.
- Empowerment works best when it is accompanied by sharing. Sharing of the entrepreneur's vision, sharing of financial information, and yes, sharing of ownership. That's empowerment with a capital E.

QUESTION 49

Q "Help! I hate firing. How can I avoid it?"

A Sorry, but you can't. You can minimize the necessity for firing by instituting effective hiring practices and targeted training programs and whiz-bang motivational techniques, but of this you can be sure . . . unless you are Mr. or Mrs. Perfect Manager, you will never be able to avoid firing. (And if you think you *are* Mr. or Mrs. Perfect Manager, it won't be long until you'll be surrounded by the kind of employees who will prove you aren't.)

But here are six time-proven and painfully learned tips to help you elevate firing a notch or two above paying income taxes or having a root canal.

1. The longer you procrastinate the actual firing, the more painful the act will be. Once the decision is made to cut the cord, get on with it.

2. Remember, you aren't the only one who recognizes underperformance; the employee recognizes it, too. He or she can't be enjoying this working experience either, and even if unwilling to acknowledge it, the quicker he or she gets on with life, the better.

3. Assuming you have a collection of capable, performing employees on the payroll, their opportunities (as well as yours) are bound to suffer because of the continuing presence of the underperformer. It's your job as team leader to put an end to everyone's suffering. Like hiring, this is one of those jobs that cannot be delegated.

4. Provide job-placement counseling for the pink-slipped employee. This counseling should be designed to help the employee get on with his or her life; at the same time, it is salving your conscience.

5. Take the afternoon off after a tough fire. Do something you enjoy . . . take in a ball game, an afternoon movie, a Mediterranean cruise.
6. Do your firing on Fridays. This gives both parties the weekend to recover.

Firing, I am sorry to say, is here to stay and is as much a part of the team-building process as is hiring, training, and motivating. Which is not to suggest we will ever come to enjoy the act, but rather that it should be approached as a fact of small business life.

Firing, like long hours and conflict resolution, is one of the prices the successful entrepreneur must pay.

PART V

Operations

The entrepreneur has had the dream, the dream has been financed, the business has evolved, and the team has been hired. What happens next?

Like the chef of a good stew, the entrepreneur must mix all those ingredients together. And if he or she mixes them correctly, lo and behold, the business's expenses will be controlled, its inventories will balance, and its receivables will turn like a well-oiled clock. Oh yes, and a spate of career opportunities will erupt for the team.

Enter the role of *operations* . . . what happens when dreams, financing, and people are blended together in pursuit of a common goal.

The common goal? To solve the customer's problems.

QUESTION 50

Q "What is *distribution?* How important is it?"

A I believe it was Confucius who once said, "He who gets it out, wins the bout." The sage old Chinese philosopher was referring, of course, to getting the product out and winning in the game of business.

Okay, so Confucius probably didn't say that, but he would have said it if he were around today and knew even the first thing about business. Small business or big business, it makes no difference, distribution (getting the product or service out) is the king. (Or queen).

So, what are the different methods of *getting it out?* They are . . .

Retail.	McDonald's retails its products. So does Wal-Mart, The Gap, and H.R. Block. In retailing, margins are bigger, but so are expenses.
Mail order.	Spiegel, L.L. Bean, and Land's End are recognizable mail order companies. Sears used to be. Mail order, similar to retail, provides good margins along with hefty expenses.
Direct Sales.	IBM, Procter & Gamble, and AT&T use direct sales forces to distribute their products. Their in-house sales staffs consist of on-the-payroll employees selling only company products.
Independent Sales Reps.	Thousands of small businesses who can't afford to maintain their own sales force use independent sales reps to distribute their products. Most independent rep groups sell more than one company's products, and are paid by a percentage of the sale.

Telemarketing.   Another form of direct sales. Usually in-house employees (although they can be independent sales reps, too), telemarketers locate, and service, their customers using the phone instead of the feet.

Network Marketing.   Network marketers utilize a web of non-employees to distribute the company's products using word-of-mouth as their primary sales tool. Amway, Shaklee, and Mary Kay Cosmetics are the most recognizable of the network marketers.

Got it? Then here's today's question. Which would you rather have if you had the choice—outstanding distribution and a mediocre product or mediocre distribution and an outstanding product?

Me? A great distribution system can move a mediocre product in the blink of an eye. Meanwhile thousands of dynamite products have never made it off the warehouse shelves, thanks to mediocre distribution.

Yes sir, right or wrong, capitalism has made the call. Distribution over product, any day.

QUESTION

Q "What's all the fuss about quality?"

A Remember small business's good old days? The days when *buyer beware* ruled the customer's purchasing decision? The days when the customer bought a product and prayed it would still be in working order by the time he got it home? The days when the Pintos and the Comets and the Gremlins roamed our city streets?

Well, those days are over. Gone. Kaput. Like it or not, the products consumers buy today have been designed and built by the Energizer bunny. They've been built to last. And last.

Or they'd better be built to last anyway, because if they aren't, the customer will take them back and demand a new one. Made by the competition. No questions asked.

And that's what all the fuss over quality is about. It's about survival. There are too many good products and services available out there, and those folks who choose to provide something else won't be around long. It's as simple as that.

Here's a collection of tips on how to help you make the quality cut.

- The commitment to quality must begin at the top. If the entrepreneur isn't willing to make an unqualified commitment, his or her employees won't be either.
- A light-hearted commitment to quality is worse than no commitment at all. Go all the way or none of the way when committing to a quality program.
- If your company doesn't have an ongoing quality program in place as we speak, you're already behind the competition. Do it

now, make the commitment to quality a part of your business strategy.

- Don't wait until the complaints hit the fan to start a quality program. The best time to start one? When things are going smoothly. That's when you'll have the most time to dedicate to its pursuit.

- It's the moments of truth that kill an entrepreneur's commitment to quality . . . those moments when the company stands face-to-face with those expensive, monumental, culture-altering decisions. Never back down.

- Quality, or the lack thereof, is not confined to the products you offer or the services you supply. Quality is everywhere. It's in the way the telephone is answered, in the way the invoices are rendered, in the way the shipments are packed. Quality is rooted in the very culture of a company. It takes long years to develop and mere days to destroy.

- Quality, by itself, will not ensure a company's success. But a lack of quality will ensure its failure.

So, how do you measure quality?

You measure it by putting yourself in your customer's shoes. How would your customers prefer to hear the telephone answered? In what format would your customers prefer their invoices rendered? In what package would your customers prefer to see their products shipped? The customer is your barometer, measuring rod, and judge, all wrapped up in one.

And remember. Today's customers have choices that yesterday's customers never had. They have taught us small business survivors a life-giving lesson: Mediocrity is no longer an acceptable way of doing business.

QUESTION

Q "What is the best way to control my expenses?"

A To answer this question you must first understand that expense control, similar to quality control, is a cultural issue. And, since it is the entrepreneur who determines a small business's culture (see Question 67), it is the entrepreneur who will determine how the company will view the spending of money and the steps that must be taken to control it.

Expenses are like weeds; they have a natural tendency to spread and to grow. Left alone, expenses won't stop spreading and growing until they overtake everything in their path, profitability included. It is the entrepreneur who must make a cast-in-stone commitment to contain his or her company's expenses and live up to fulfilling that commitment.

Once that cast-in-stone commitment to control expenses has been made, here are some tips on how to make it happen.

1. *Zero-base budgeting.* It isn't enough to want to cut expenses; there must also be a system or method to make it happen. Zero-base budgeting to the rescue.

   Zero-base budgeting works like this. You assume that, at the beginning of each budgeting year, your individual expense accounts are absolute zero, like they would be if you were starting the company from scratch. Then question every dollar budgeted to every line item. (In other words, yesterday's expenses are not necessarily today's.)

   It's a time consuming process when compared to the traditional way of budgeting expenses (i.e., adding a cost-of-living percentage to last year's expenses). Cost of living up 5 percent? Zap, zap, add 5 percent to last year's expenses. Easy, quick, and oh so ineffective.

Yes, zero-base budgeting is worth the additional effort. Unlike sales where (if you're lucky) ten cents of every dollar filters down to the bottom line, every penny of a shaved expense ends up in your company's pocket. Those business gurus who preach *reengineering* know, expense cutting is the most efficient method of increasing profitability.

2. *Recognize that the need for expense control is forever.* Twenty years ago, strict control of expenses was an option. No longer, thanks to such factors as foreign competition, technology advances, and consumer awareness. Yes, today American business is on a fat free diet, and will remain that way, throughout our lifetime anyway.

3. *Put the responsibility for controlling expenses where it belongs.* Control of expenses isn't the job of the CEO, the accounting department, or the purchasing department. It's the job of the employees, the teams, or the departments who consume those expense dollars.

   Make those who are responsible accountable.

4. *Don't wait until a crisis arrives.* Institute an expense control program now, when things are going well; when you have the time and the energy to make the system work.

   Don't be one of those who must be motivated by fear before you act. Instead, be one of those who are motivated by efficiency.

5. *Avoid over-staffing.* Once you've hired an employee it's difficult and expensive to un-hire him. Use outside contractors and part-timers whenever possible.

6. *Technology is cheaper than people.* Purchase user-friendly software in lieu of accumulating additional employees. Areas such as accounting and bookkeeping, inventory control, accounts receivable, and payroll lend themselves to software. Wherever possible, let technology, not people, do the detail work.

7. *Recognize and reward.* The best way to develop an expense-aware culture is to publicly recognize those who are responsible for controlling the expenses, and reward them once they've done their job.

And finally, remember that expense control is not only a profitability issue, it is also an important element of controlling cash flow. And, since lack of cash is the number one symptom of small business failure, how better to begin building a solid foundation than to begin by controlling expenses?

QUESTION 53

Q "Are meetings really necessary? How can I improve my company's meetings?"

A Meetings are an American institution, like hamburgers, french fries, and Monday Night Football. A much maligned American institution, however. From big business to small business to the PTA, everybody goes to, but nobody likes, meetings.

However . . .

1. Meetings are a necessary element of running a business, and yet;
2. Meetings take valuable time away from their participants, and thus;
3. Good meetings take less of their participant's valuable time than bad meetings, and unfortunately;
4. There are more bad meetings than good meetings, and finally;
5. Anyone can have good meetings, but most of us unwittingly make the decision to have bad ones.

Study other businesses. It won't take you long to learn that a company that runs its meetings efficiently also treats its customers efficiently, trains its employees efficiently, and ships its products efficiently. As a matter of fact, a company that runs its meetings efficiently also runs its entire business efficiently. You will soon understand . . . efficiency is a cultural issue and a mindset, and well-run meetings are only one of the results of that mindset.

How about your company? Do you run your meetings efficiently? (If not, why don't you? The choice is yours, you know.)

Here are a collection of tips on how to upgrade the efficiency of your meetings, for those of you who will make the conscious decision to do so. (My guarantee: Improved meetings will result in improved planning, enhanced execution, and enriched profitability.)

TIPS ON IMPROVING MEETINGS

1. *Always ask the question in advance, can this meeting be avoided?* Could the same purpose be served by a hallway gathering, a brief stop in someone's office, or a spur-of-the-moment pow-wow? It's a fact . . . meetings are expensive and most companies have too many of them.

2. *Just how expensive are your meetings?*   Know the answer to this question before you call one. Multiply the number of people attending by the average hourly wage (including benefits). Be sure to include the time wasted on either end of the meeting. (Believe it or not, there is software available to perform this cost-of-the-meeting task for you.)

   Knowing the cost of your meetings will motivate you to control the frequency of them, as well as to ensure that only the necessary participants attend.

3. *Maximize preparation.*   Send out a meeting announcement at least one day in advance of the meeting. Identify the participants and let them know the time, place, and subject. Knowing the subject in advance will give the attendees plenty of time to consider the issues, thus improving their chances to contribute.

4. *Minimize surprises.*   Surprises tend to startle and confuse, both of which detract from the purpose of a meeting.

5. *Choose attendees with care.*   The more people at the meeting, the longer it takes to reach a conclusion. Or stated another way, the usefulness of most problem-solving or creative meetings is inversely proportional to the size of the group.

   When in doubt, leave 'em out.

6. *Start the meeting on time.*   And end it on time. Remember, people (yourself included) must plan the rest of their day around this meeting.

7. *Every meeting should have a facilitator.*   At the outset of the meeting, it is the facilitator's responsibility to state the purpose of

the meeting, along with any goals. The facilitator is also responsible for keeping the meeting on track, making sure no single person dominates the discussions, and insuring that a logical conclusion is reached.

8. *Don't allow interruptions.* If a meeting can be interrupted, it isn't important enough to be a meeting.

9. *Quicker and shorter is always better.* Meetings are no exception.

10. *Save the best news for the last.* End the meeting on an upkick.

11. *The facilitator should send a review of the just-concluded meeting to all participants.* Outline the decisions reached and the responsibilities assigned.

12. *Never hold meetings on Monday mornings or Friday afternoons.* Too many better things to do on Monday mornings and too many distractions on Friday afternoons.

13. *Take an inventory.* Are you spending too much time in meetings? More than 25 percent? Then something is wrong—with you and/or your organization. Review your company's regularly scheduled meetings, recognizing that meetings can be habit forming. Cull those meetings that have outgrown their usefulness.

You say your company is having a problem with meetings? Too many and too inefficient? Well, I'd be willing to bet your company is having other problems, too. Problems returning phone calls promptly, and finishing important projects on time, and respecting other employee's time.

How do I know? Because poor meetings are just another way of abusing people's time. If your company is abusing people's time through its meetings, you are most likely abusing it by not returning phone calls, handing in late projects, and by not respecting people's time.

The good news? We're not talking about an uncontrollable event here. We're talking about an internal problem, one that can be resolved through conscious effort.

Conscious effort that begins at the top. With you.

QUESTION 54

Q **"My company isn't big enough to afford a full-time secretary. What should I do about all the duties a secretary performs?"**

A Let's recount some of the typical secretary's services.

- *Manages time, maintains appointments, keeps calendars.* Computer software is available that can do all three. Faster and better, too. (Computers don't take vacations, disappear into restrooms, or hang out at copy machines.)
- *Manages telephone calls.* A combination of voice mail and E-mail can do the same thing. Quicker, too, and with more accurate recall.
- *Types letters and memos.* Word processing is a snap these days. Just learn how to finger a keyboard and the memos will fly.
- *Filing.* Maintain your own computer files (your computer will do it for you), then farm out the rest to a bookkeeper or clerk.
- *Details.* Keep them to a minimum, pay attention to those you can't avoid, and farm out the wee ones. (Hey, if Sam Walton could mind his millions of details, you can mind your thousands.)

So what am I getting at here? I steadfastly maintain that, in lieu of a secretary . . .

Every entrepreneur should have his or her own PC!

Not a CRT with access to inventory and receivables mind you, but his or her own PC with his or her own confidential access. And on that PC every entrepreneur should maintain an E-mail account for those folks (employees, vendors, and customers) who need to communicate both frequently and accurately.

Every entrepreneur should also have a spread sheet on that PC. And on that spread sheet should be an up-to-date profit and loss statement along with an up-to-date balance sheet. Thus, every time there's a significant change in one or the other (a large capital expenditure, a major unscheduled expense, a one-time profitability blip, and so on) in between regular financial reporting periods, our wired-in entrepreneur can pull up his or her current financials, plug in the significant change, and see how it flows through.

And finally, every entrepreneur should do his or her own word processing (secretary or no secretary). Cranking out your own memos, for instance, is faster than the old-fashioned dictating, rereading, and signing routine. It's also less expensive and more confidential.

A down-the-road bonus to having your own PC and doing your own word processing? Once you become a finger-flying processor of words, you can pursue a new and unique career when your entrepreneurial fires burn out.

Like writing books.
Like me.

QUESTION

Q "Should I utilize strict rules and regulations in managing my company?"

A That depends. If you're talking about managing people, hopefully you've learned . . . people, like horses, can be led to water but they can't be made to drink. People drink on their own volition.

And so it is with strict rules and regulations. Never overly fond of them, people act on their own volition. Sometimes they fall in line, and even enjoy rules and regulations. Most often they don't. It's only been in the last few years that management practices have caught on to the fact: Business isn't war, people aren't marionettes, and latitude breeds attitude, in a nonhostile working environment anyway. Maybe General Patton and his unbending rules and regulations have a place in the world, but it isn't in small business. Not any more anyway. Not the way employees are today.

Sorry, but strict rules and regulations are out where managing people is concerned. That's because people come in too many sizes, shapes, and forms, and have too many warts and blemishes, too many idiosyncrasies. Today's employees need a flexible framework in which to work; one that allows them to zig when they need to zig, zag when they need to zag.

Take people out of the management formula, however, and strict rules and regulations are in. Asset management, for instance, requires a myriad of strict rules and regulations. That's because buildings and machines aren't crafted from cells and cellulose, but rather from bricks and mortar, and bricks and mortar respond to rote and consistency. Ditto with a host of other management issues, such as expense control (the tighter the fist, the better), quality control (mediocrity is out), and substance abuse (no flexibility here).

So, what does all this mean to small business? It means that if a good employee has a family emergency, rules or no rules, he or she can walk out the door in the middle of the day. It means that if a good customer needs a widget this afternoon, rules or no rules, that good customer gets his widget this afternoon. And it means that if a good vendor needs to be paid in advance, rules or no rules, that good vendor gets paid in advance.

Yes, rules and regulations have their place in the management formula, but not when it comes to managing people.

QUESTION

Q "My physical inventories never balance with my book inventories. Why?"

A Before I answer that question, here's some advice for those of you who are still on the small business sidelines, watching, waiting, trying to make up your mind.

Personally, I prefer rattlesnakes to inventory. Rattlesnakes are less dangerous. You can hear rattlesnakes coming, you can see them as they prepare to strike, and you can beat them to death with a stick.

Not so with inventory. Inventory is a cash-sucking, profit-draining, silent killer. It just sits there and collects dust. And interest. It doesn't rattle or hiss or threaten, it just gets older, and yellower, and deadlier. And then its detail-despising owner finally discovers that all of his or her cash is tied up in shelf after shelf of dusty, obsolete inventory, with nothing left over for paying the bills. Whereupon the creditors move in and the employees move out and all that dusty, obsolete inventory brings the house down.

My advice, especially if you aren't one of those folks who simply love details? Find an inventoryless business. One without racks and shelves and forklifts. Sell a service instead, or peddle someone else's inventory from a far-away factory. Or become a consultant, or a writer, or an automobile mechanic. Do anything—just stay out of inventory's way.

You say you can't avoid inventory? Okay, then smother it in details.

Back to the original question. Here are a number of reasons why your physical inventory might not balance with your books.

1. You've got too much of it. Mass breeds mess.
2. You don't have the right support system (hardware, software, and/or people).
3. Something is wrong with your receiving department. The system is wrong or the people are wrong. Or both.
4. Something is wrong with your shipping department. Ditto above.
5. You don't take physical inventories often enough. Mistakes accumulate and trails get old.
6. The physical inventories you do take aren't accurate enough. Again, systems or people shortcomings, or both.
7. Something is wrong with your inventory evaluation system (costing). That's right—systems or people problems, or both.

So, how do you solve these problems?

1. *Too much inventory?* Upgrade (train and/or motivate and/or replace) whoever it is that is responsible for the purchasing. That's where most too-much-inventory problems begin.
2. *Wrong support system?* Review the accounting system. Replace or upgrade the hardware or software that processes the information. Replace or upgrade the people accountable.
3. *Receiving department problems?* Replace or upgrade the receiving system and replace or upgrade the people responsible for managing and staffing it.
4. *Shipping department problems?* Ditto #3.
5. *Not enough physical inventories?* Take more. Always quarterly. Even more often if necessary, until the problem is solved.
6. *Inaccurate physicals?* Upgrade or replace your physical inventory system. Taking a physical inventory isn't a rocket-science task, but it is a detail-ridden, time-consuming, drudgery-filled chore.
7. *Inventory evaluation?* Upgrade or replace the costing system.

And so it goes in the business of managing inventory. The responsibilities inherent in handling it never end.

What does end is the small business that doesn't handle its inventory with care.

QUESTION 57

Q "What are accounts receivable? How can I improve mine?"

A Accounts receivable (aka *receivables*) represent our hard earned cash languishing in someone else's bank account. Hard earned cash that could be used to reduce debt or to pay bills or to finance new sales. All other things being equal, the smaller the small business's accounts receivables (in relation to sales), the healthier the small business's financial condition.

Every successful small business needs someone dedicated to the collection of receivables. In the early stages of the business, that someone is usually the entrepreneur. In later stages that responsibility may be delegated to a bookkeeper, comptroller, or chief financial officer (CFO). But whoever that delagee is, he or she must be passionate about collecting monies due the business; first politely following up, then relentlessly hounding, and finally hauling the deadbeats to court.

After all, accounts receivable are cash and cash keeps the doors open and nobody messes with a successful small business's cash!

Today's business logic *deifies* the customer, and well it should. After all, someone has to step to the plate and purchase our products or services. But the word *customer* is incomplete, the correct phrase should be *paying customer*. The successful entrepreneurs among us have learned: A customer is not a customer until he (or she) pays their bill.

Here are a collection of hard-earned tips on how to keep your accounts receivable in line with your sales.

- *What gets measured gets attention.* Outstanding receivables should be *aged* (the computation of the average age of all receivables) at least once a month. This aging list should sit on the entrepreneur's desk right next to the telephone, a constant reminder of who is in temporary control of the company's cash. An acceptable receivable age (in most industries) is 40 days. Danger signals should appear once a receivable exceeds 45 days.

- *Not everyone is a desired customer.* Only those customers who pay their bills on time are *desired customers*. Don't bet the house on hot-shot customers who promise big purchases. Make sure those customers can also pay.

- *Check credit.* You can bet that your good vendors checked on your credit; you should check on your customers', too. Remember, the granting of credit is a privilege. In effect, you are loaning money to your customers. Grant credit with care.

- *Establish terms.* No sale should be made without first establishing credit terms. Terms should work for both parties, but remember, when a customer wants you to carry his receivables for long periods of time, that's your signature on the bank's guarantee. Your bank won't back off its terms, why should you?

- *Credit application.* Design and use a credit application. Every potential customer should fill one out.

- *Evaluate all applicants.* Ask yourself these three questions before approving a credit application: Does this applicant have the ability to pay? Have they indicated by their past actions a willingness to pay on time? Can you make a reasonable profit on this account? If the answer to any of these questions is no, cede this customer to your competition.

- *Signed contract.* Design a boilerplate sales contract, one that provides the legalese you need to collect your monies in court. Outline everything from payment terms to late payment charges to collection procedures. Officially signed sales contracts denote professionalism, and potential deadbeats usually pay the professionals first.

- *Financial statement.* Don't be afraid to ask for a financial statement before shipping a first-time customer. Remember, you are providing your customer a product in exchange for a promise to pay. Thus, a receivable is a loan, and most loans require financial statements.

- *Up-front money.* When in doubt, ask for money up front. Professional customers will understand the request (though they may not agree to it). The potential deadbeats will huff and puff and take their undesirable business elsewhere.

- *The older the receivable the less likely to pay.* Don't wait until your receivables are over 90 days to kick in your collection procedure. Do it while the invoice is still warm (45 days or sooner).
- *Use a collection agency only as a last resort.* Collection agencies are expensive (up to 50 percent of the receivable). Also, collection agencies are not known to be delicate in dealing with deadbeats, so you can kiss that customer good-bye.
- *Utilize a carrying charge or delinquency charge.* You are expected to pay something extra when you extend your payment terms (review your VISA agreement if you have any doubts). Your customers should, too.
- *No-pay, no-ship.* Don't ship to ongoing customers who consistently don't pay on time. After all, your good vendors wouldn't ship to you if you didn't pay on time. In those cases where you determine you absolutely, positively, *must* have the slow-pay's business, be sure to build the cost of carrying the receivables into the sales price.

Remember, receivables represent cash and cash is liquidity. The liquid small business has a smorgasbord of options.

The nonliquid business has only one.

QUESTION 58

Q "I want to increase my company's profits. Where do I begin?"

A   Increasing profits can result from any one of three activities: decreasing expenses, increasing margins, or increasing revenues (sales).

A discussion of each follows.

DECREASING EXPENSES

Always the first place to look for new profit dollars and always the least risky to implement. For immediate results, begin with those expense accounts that can be most easily affected. For instance, there are always quick and easy dollars to be found in such categories as travel and entertainment, utilities, insurance, and whatever your compost account is entitled (miscellaneous?). Then move on to the more difficult, but also most highly leveraged expense accounts . . . especially those that include salaries, wages, and benefits. Big dollars await those who are willing to muddy these sacrosanct waters, but beware, big conflict looms nearby, too. Be steadfast but be careful.

Another reason to head for expenses first? That's where the leverage is. Every expense dollar eliminated tumbles headlong to the bottom line. Every single one.

There is a bonus that comes from an expense-cutting program. Expense control is a cultural issue and one giant step has just been taken towards creating a cost-conscious culture. Once a tight-fisted culture is installed, the hard work will be over. The culture will maintain itself.

INCREASING MARGIN

There are two ways to increase margin; the first is by increasing prices, the second by decreasing cost of goods sold. Significant dollars can be found in both.

As simple as it may sound, an increase in price does not come without its downsides. Sales volume will probably pay the price as low-balling customers take their business elsewhere. Will you miss them? Probably not! Often they are the same folks who beat you up on delivery and take 90 days to pay their bills.

Decreasing cost of goods sold can be an easier and less dangerous approach. Usually this process involves either seeking price reductions and/or better service from current suppliers or finding new suppliers with lower prices and/or better service. (And don't forget the *incoming freight* account; there are plenty of excess-dollars-without-offsetting-costs to be found there, too).

INCREASING REVENUES (SALES)

Aha, finally the fun part, for most entrepreneurs anyway. Increasing revenues includes the hiring of new sales people, the introduction of new products, the uncovering of new markets. The kinds of things most entrepreneurs are bred to do.

But adding revenues does not come without adding risk. There are real and tangible costs involved. Salespeople must be hired and trained, new products developed and introduced, new markets located, and most of all, a new infrastructure must be introduced to handle the increased sales volume.

And remember, when planning your sales push, not every sale is a profitable sale—there are good ones and there are bad ones. Good sales are to customers who are willing to pay a fair price and willing to pay their bills on your terms. Bad sales are to customers who are unwilling to pay a fair price and unwilling to pay their bills on your terms.

The correct way to make a push to increase profitability? In the order outlined above—first, make a beeline for expenses, then attack margin, and finally, pursue increased sales. Don't dive into all three at once and don't expect to achieve the desired results by yourself. Involve the team in the effort, set goals for everyone, focus on what you can reasonably achieve, and broadcast and reward the progress you make.

QUESTION 59

Q *"Can my company grow too fast?"*

A Close your eyes. Picture a drunken driver hurtling down the highway, his car laden with passengers and moving too fast to effectively steer. The car and its hapless passengers are at the mercy of fate—the next curve in the road could be the last.

And so it is with a small business that is moving too fast. The entrepreneur, intoxicated with his or her early success, has the business moving too fast to effectively steer, as it hurtles down the small business pike, outrunning its infrastructure. Similar to the out-of-control car, the business is at the mercy of the next curve in its road.

Yes, a small business *can* grow too fast. As a matter of fact, too-rapid-growth is one of the entrepreneur's most dangerous enemies. It is a silent and unannounced killer and it preys on us entrepreneurs as a result of our unbridled optimism. Because of the rose-colored glasses we wear, its stealthy approach is seldom noticed until it's too late.

The final throes of a company that has grown too fast are usually related to cash, or more specifically, to the lack of it. But before the coffers run completely dry, the tell-tale results of growing too fast will appear in a variety of forms.

- *Unhappy customers.* The small business that grows too fast doesn't have the time or the energy to treat its customers the way customers need to be treated. The complaints will be many and varied, and the juiciest ones will always end up smack dab in the middle of the entrepreneur's desk.
- *Unhappy employees.* There isn't enough time to solve employee problems because the entrepreneur is too busy reacting to the

latest crisis. Solutions to ongoing employee dilemmas come last or not at all.

- *Straining systems and controls.*   Issues such as inventory management, quality control, and financial systems crash and burn. The company has outgrown the ones in place but it doesn't have the time, the energy, or the cash to create and install the right ones.

- *The entrepreneur's time.*   More and more of the entrepreneur's time is spent huddling with his or her financial people, bankers, or lawyers, rather than brainstorming with the company's sales, marketing, or production people. Fire fighting is the order of the day.

- *Entrepreneurial burnout.*   More and more of the entrepreneur's Saturdays are spent just about anywhere but the office. Work isn't fun anymore.

The problem? Sales growth is the entrepreneur's aphrodisiac. Not profitability growth, opportunity growth, or equity growth, but sales growth. We entrepreneurs gleefully answer the question, "How big is your company?" with the size of its sales.

"Sold one million dollars last year!" we proudly boast—never mind that we can't pay our bills. "Ten million dollars and growing!" we crow happily—although we haven't made a profit in years.

Sorry, but sales is the means to an end, not the end. The true end? Profitability. Only profitability should define us, and the "how big is your company" question should be answered by return on sales, not by sales itself. Or by return on equity, or by return on investment, or by absolute profitability dollars. Not by gross sales.

Bigger, you see, isn't necessarily better, in the small business world anyway.

Only better is better.

QUESTION 60

Q "How can I ensure that my company grows at a manageable pace?"

A Every business goes through a series of predictable stages of growth. The early years of a company's existence are known as the entrepreneurial years and are characterized by the energy and direction of the entrepreneur. From there, the business moves into its norming years, as the business achieves profitability and some degree of order. And finally, the business tumbles headlong into the integrating years, that period of time when the now mature company either makes the necessary changes to restart the life cycle or, if it doesn't, it exits the business world permanently. (For more on small business life cycles, see my first book, *The Brass Tacks Entrepreneur.*)

Within those stages of predictable growth, the small business can either experience unhealthy growth or healthy growth. Unhealthy growth occurs when sales soar while infrastructure plods. Healthy growth occurs when sales and infrastructure grow together in healthy tandem.

To ensure healthy growth, most entrepreneurs must first make an attitudinal adjustment. They must shake the typical entrepreneur's sales mentality, and understand that growth doesn't come from sales alone (see Question 59). Growth must come from everywhere, and sales is only one of those everywheres. Without all of the everywheres working together, sales growth isn't true growth; it is only trouble waiting to happen.

Once the entrepreneur's attitudinal adjustment is made, here is what must be done to ensure healthy growth.

1. *Control sales.*   Don't hire new salespeople, establish new sales territories, or introduce new products, until an infrastructure capable of digesting them is in place. The elements of this *digesting* process include the availability of cash, the upgrading of internal systems and controls, and the development of the administration and operation teams.

2. *Earnings must keep pace with sales.*   In the long term, earnings must keep pace with sales. Otherwise the dreaded cash flow problem is bound to raise its ugly head. It's a fact that's been proven many times; the problems caused by growing receivables and expanding inventory can bring a business to its knees just as quickly as any bank work-out department.

   A competent financial person can determine, by juggling several key figures, exactly what earnings growth is required to fund and sustain the desired sales growth rate. Then, once it has been determined that the necessary earnings growth rate is not being sustained, the growth of sales can be curtailed. (Curtailing sales is a lot easier than creating them.)

3. *Systems and controls must keep pace with sales.*   Healthy growth requires, among a long list of organizational issues, paperwork systems, inventory management systems, and financial accounting systems, as well as effective management control over each. These systems and controls need to change as the company grows, and the savvy entrepreneur soon learns that change is the order of every small business person's day. What worked a year ago won't necessarily work today.

4. *Team members must keep pace with sales.*   The small business's number one asset is its people, and if the team doesn't grow at the same rate (or faster) than its sales, it will be the customers who ultimately pay. To be followed by the business itself.

   And how does the team keep up with expanding sales? Through training and motivating, all provided at the insistence and beneficence of the company's number one trainer and motivator, the entrepreneur. (Who had better, incidentally, be keeping up with the pace of sales, too).

The primary lesson for those of us who worship growth: It is sometimes necessary to speed up by slowing down.

QUESTION

Q "What is cash flow? Why is it so important?"

A Cash is a fuel. It is like the sunshine that keeps the trees growing, the water that keeps the turbines churning, the diesel that keeps the locomotives chugging. It is the sustenance that keeps every business, big or small, private or public, profitable or unprofitable, operating. Every business needs a positive flow of cash to keep the doors open.

No positive flow of cash? No doors to open, no products to sell, and no one to sell them.

One of the entrepreneur's primary duties is to ensure that the positive flow of cash is maintained. If the flow of cash is positive, the business will run without interruption. If the flow is negative, it will come to a screeching halt.

The inflow and outflow of cash comes from a variety of sources.

INFLOW

- Cash sales.
- Collection of receivables.
- New investment capital.
- New loans.
- Sale of fixed assets.

OUTFLOW

- Accounts payable (for the purchase of everything from inventory to assets).

148

- Taxes payable.
- Payroll.
- Dividends, interest, and loan pay-offs.
- All operating expenses.

More cash coming in than cash going out? Positive cash flow.
More cash going out than coming in? Negative cash flow.

This concept of cash flow incidentally, must not be confused with the concept of profitability. Profitability is a long-term, over-an-accounting-period-of-time issue, while cash flow is a today, life-or-death matter. The small business keeps its bankers and shareholders happy with profitability; it keeps its employees and suppliers happy (and its doors open) with cash.

Don't be misled by accounting terminology. A profitable business is quite capable of developing cash flow problems, too. For instance, if that business's profits are used to purchase more inventory than the company needs, or if its profits are used to purchase more assets than the company can utilize, or if its profits are tied up in receivables that won't turn into cash in a reasonable amount of time, then a negative cash flow condition will result, profitability or no.

The management of cash involves the management of details. Details that include entrepreneurially unfriendly chores such as the on-time collecting of receivables, the efficient managing of inventory, and the day-to-day juggling of payables. Managing cash is a penny-pinching business, and to the best penny-pincher goes cash's spoils.

Obviously, a workable cash flow forecasting system is an important element of managing cash flow (see Question 26), and the development of an efficient projection system takes years to perfect. Yet, a week should never go by without creating and reviewing the latest set of cash flow projections (except that is, when cash gets tight, in which case a *day* should never go by).

Me? If I had it to do all over again, I'd start tracking my company's cash flow the same day I opened its first checking account.

Q "What do I do when my company gets into trouble?"

A   A sick small business doesn't suddenly become a healthy small business with a shot of penicillin and a few days in bed. Instead, a series of drastic changes is required, and the first of those changes must be with the doctor. That's you. After all, it was you who prescribed the company into this mess, and it is you who must prescribe it out.

And so, face the facts. The primary problem when your business falters isn't the actions of your employees, your customers, or the economy. The primary problem is you. And your business doesn't need more of the same prescription that you got here; it needs a dose of something new.

Your company needs you to make a change. A strategic change.

To make a strategic change you must first take an inventory. Identify those attitudes and skills of yours that need changing. Don't worry if you can't put your finger on them—your employees can. As well as your spouse, your mentor, your board of directors, your shareholders, and anyone else who works closely with you.

From that inventory select those areas you are capable of changing. Then either make the designated changes, hire someone to make them for you, or pick up the phone and call your lawyer. Your problems are about to get worse.

After you've faced your need to make a strategic change, identified the attitudes and skills that need changing, and commit yourself to making those changes.

Here are some tips on places to begin.

1. *If you aren't tracking cash flow, now is the time.*   When a company is in trouble, cash will be either its savior or its killer. It's time you understand its habits and haunts.

2. *Don't throw more sales at the problem.*   Most entrepreneurs rely on sales to get them out of trouble, but more sales only increases the need for cash which, in turn, only compounds the problems. Instead, focus your attention and energy where the problems exist (i.e., operations, administration, or personnel), and solve those problems first. Leave sales for last.

3. *Full disclosure begets full cooperation.*   Don't attempt to cover-up your problems. The word of your woes will eventually leak out and the people you need as allies (your employees, bankers, and shareholders) will feel like outsiders.

4. *Work with your creditors.*   Let your vendors know what you're doing to work your way out of your problems. Most vendors would prefer to work with you instead of against you. After all, it's in their best interest that you survive.

5. *Investigate what a bankruptcy filing (Chapter 11) can do for you.* Bankruptcy has its place in the capitalistic system, and has rescued many an ailing small business. Don't let your pride stand in the way.

6. *When all else fails, hire a turn-around expert.*   You may not like what they'll do, and whatever they do will be painful, but these folks are the doctor's doctors. The good ones have stopped bleedings worse than yours.

Like children, every small business is bound to get sick; it is an integral part of the process of growing up. The difference between terminal illness or complete recovery will be the doctor and the medicine he or she prescribes.

That doctor is you. Your medicine is change.

QUESTION

Q "What are my options when I get in over my head?"

A If this was a perfect world, you wouldn't get in over your head. Instead you'd become another Bill Gates and your small business would grow into a big business and soar off to unscaled heights. And before you could say the words, "initial public offering" (IPO), your symbol would tick across the New York Stock Exchange board, your products would become a household word, and you would make more money than a Wall Street Banker.

This isn't a perfect world. You, like most of the rest of us, *will* get in over your head. And not just a little over your head, either. When this situation occurs, your options are to:

1. *Go back to the drawing board and reengineer yourself and your company.* Make the necessary personal, managerial, and strategic business changes necessary to resume your company's growth (see Questions 60, 87, and 88). Usually the toughest of the available options, but in most cases the one with the most leverage.

2. *Hire a president, CEO, or COO.* Or whatever you wish to call the person who will run your business on a day-to-day basis and who will possess the managerial skills that you don't have. Make sure, however, that your company can afford the right individual (the good ones don't come cheaply), and make sure you can keep your mouth shut when he or she does things differently than you. Remember, you aren't hiring a puppet, you're hiring a president. You don't want repetition, you want innovation.

3. *Hire a turnaround expert.*   Expensive? Yes. Worth the expense? Usually (if you've hired the right one). Painless? Absolutely not—you won't like many of the things they do or the way they do them (bowing to tradition is not one of their favorite pastimes).

Is hiring a turnaround expert your last resort? Almost. Only two options remain. They are . . .

4. *Sell the business.*   There are other niches out there, waiting to be discovered. Perhaps it's time you began discovering them.

5. *Continue to do things exactly the way you've been doing them.*   Or, stated another way, go down for the third, and last, time.

QUESTION

Q "How will I know when it's time to sell my business?"

A There are two reasons entrepreneurs decide to sell their businesses. One is because they *want to* (something else looks better) and the second is because they *have to* (the businesses' days are numbered). The former is preferable, the latter is all too common.

Aside from the obvious problems that erupt with increasing frequency each day at the office, how will you know when your small business days are numbered?

Don't worry, you'll know, and the message won't come from your head, it will come from your heart.

In the form of burnout. Entrepreneurial burnout.

Entrepreneurial burnout is the result of one, or a combination of several, entrepreneurially unfriendly emotions, each guaranteed to change the way you view your once-revered business. Once these unfriendly emotions have taken over, no longer is your office your favorite place to be. Now it's your bed. No longer are your employees your nearest and dearest friends. Now it's your golf foursome. No longer is your business on your mind all of the time. Now it's your family, or your friends, or your lawn that needs moving.

These entrepreneurially unfriendly emotions include:

- *Boredom.* You've been doing the same thing for umpteen years and you're sick of it. It's time to move on.
- *Curiosity.* Your eyes have suddenly opened. There's a world marching by, and you've been too busy to join the parade. You yearn to do something else.
- *Fear.* Interest rates have soared. Sales have softened. New competitors have attacked. Oh yes, and *that* bank is making

unfriendly noises again. Your silver lining has suddenly turned gray.

- *Loneliness.*   You're *IT* in your working environment, and your shoulders are sagging from too many years of last-stop responsibility. You yearn to walk into someone's office and dump *your* problems on *their* desk. Just once.

Once one or more of these unfriendly emotions have secured a foothold in your heart, burnout is just around the corner. And when it arrives, there is only one place to go.

Away. Far away.

QUESTION 65

Q "Once I've decided to sell, what's next?"

A The prospective seller's first duty is to make absolutely, positively sure, beyond any reasonable doubt, that when that point-of-no-return moment comes, he or she is prepared to sign the papers and walk away. There must be no second thoughts, no *seller's remorse* lingering in his or her mind.

Seller's remorse is an expensive and dangerous disease, and one that is peculiar to founding entrepreneurs. Expensive because it costs big dollars to undo the sales process once it is set in motion, and dangerous because of the message that the tentative sale has sent to the company's employees.

Once, however, the decision to sell has been absolutely, positively made, the rest of the process is relatively easy. Hire a credible broker (just like you would if you were selling a parcel of real estate), include a lawyer in all major decisions, and let the two of them lead you through the process.

So how do you find a credible business broker? The same way you find a credible lawyer, accountant, or consultant. You network to find viable candidates, interview more than one, interview a second time, gather references, check those references religiously, and, once all that has been done, negotiate the details of the relationship.

Here are several of the key issues your business broker and lawyer will help you resolve as you prepare to sell your business.

- *Price determination.* The selling price of a small business is usually determined using a price/earnings ratio process (i.e., a multiplier of past earnings). On some occasions it can also be arrived at by determining the value of assets and then attaching a *blue sky* factor to that value . . . a number you believe your business is worth over and above the assets. Or, in situations when past earnings and total assets are negligible, an *opportunity price* may be used (a figure based on what the right buyer would be capable of earning with the business).

Most business brokers will advise the seller to retain a *valuation professional* whose job, as the name implies, is to determine the value of small businesses. Valuation professionals will, for a price (usually somewhere between $5,000 and $15,000), prepare a detailed report for the seller.

- *Terms.*   How much cash do you need from the deal and how much seller financing are you agreeable to carry? Most buyers of small businesses will seek as much seller financing as possible, and some will demand a long-term note as part of the deal. You must have an idea going in of how much cash you will need and how much seller financing you are willing to grant.

- *Buyer credibility.*   Since most sales of small businesses include seller financing, the buyer's ability to make a success of the ongoing business, and thus continue making payments on the note, is of primary concern to the seller.

- *Personal or business guarantees.*   Sellers want the personal guarantees of buyers, while buyers prefer to guarantee only the assets of the business. The negotiated answer will often lie somewhere in between.

- *Selling stock or assets?*   It is to the seller's advantage to sell stock, the buyer's advantage to buy assets. The tax implications are huge, this should be an important element of the negotiating process.

- *Due diligence.*   Due diligence, otherwise known as the discovery process, is the purchaser's antidote to *let the buyer beware.* In most cases the more professional the buyer, the more thorough the due diligence process will be. Be prepared to answer tough questions, to have old skeletons unearthed, and to have all your warts and blemishes uncovered in the discovery process.

  Don't get your feathers ruffled by the demands of the due diligence process. After all, wouldn't you perform the same intense scrutiny if you were considering buying your business?

- *Communications with employees.*   The selling process is, in most cases, traumatic to old-line employees, and the resumes will begin to fly as soon as the rumors emerge. It is of utmost importance that the release of information regarding the sale be properly timed and carefully managed.

- *The seller's role in the surviving business.*   What will be the seller's role after the deal is done? The options are either to wave a friendly good-bye to the old business or to remain employed for a designated period of time under an employment contract.

And finally, a word to the wise from someone who has learned his *business-selling* lessons the hard way. Realize, whether or not you're included as a member of the surviving business's management, that things are about to change in your old business, and not just a little. The new owner will come to the table with a new culture in hand, and well that new owner should. After all, he or she has paid (hopefully dearly) for the right.

Your role? Swallow it or step aside. There's no middle ground.

PART VI

Culture

Every organization has a culture; good, bad, or indifferent. Nations, cities, and Wednesday night bowling teams have cultures, too.

Culture is the way things are done around here. It is the consistency of a quarter pounder, the smile on a Nordstrom sales clerk's face, the spotless appearance of a Disneyland or a Disneyworld.

Nothing escapes culture's grasp.

QUESTION

Q "What is *culture?* Why is it so important?"

A Culture, the dictionary tells us, is defined as "the ideas, customs, skills, and arts, of a people or group that are transferred, communicated, or passed along to succeeding generations."

Sounds okay, Mr. Webster, but here are several additional definitions of culture that can be specifically adapted to a small business.

- Culture is a company's value system.
- Culture is a company's personality.
- Culture is behavior, handed down from one employee to the next.
- Culture is unwritten law, defining what's done and what isn't done.
- Culture is *the way things are done around here.*

Whichever definition you choose, every company has its culture whether the company knows it or likes it. That culture is tangible and real, is established by the actions of the entrepreneur, and begins on his or her first day on the job and ends on his or her last.

A company's culture is a make-it-or-break-it element of success, because it, more than any collection of rules, regulations, or company policies, guides the behavior of all employees, including the entrepreneur. There aren't enough pages in the employee handbook to dictate an employee's actions in the myriad situations that are presented to him or her each day.

Culture fills in the blanks.

QUESTION 67

Q "How do I influence the development of my company's culture?"

A Entrepreneurs influence the development of their company's culture the same way parents influence the development of their children: by the examples they set. Not by what they say, but by what they do.

The culture of a small business is a reflection of its owner. (Don't worry; this doesn't mean your employees must have your red hair, but it does mean they had better share your ethics, values, and work habits.) Which means that if you work at a feverish pace, your employees will, too. If you insist on perfection, your employees will, too. If you growl at customers, your employees will, too.

See what I mean? You establish the culture, your employees live it.

Why? Because we entrepreneurs create and build our teams of employees in our own image. We hire the kind of employees we like, and then we promote those who act and perform in a manner acceptable to us. Soon we've collected an entire company filled with folks who act and perform like we want them to act and perform. And then we reward those who behave in our image, and we punish those who don't.

That's how a culture develops, and that's how it's maintained. The entrepreneur's actions don't speak louder than words in the culture-setting business—they speak by themselves.

QUESTION 68

Q "What are the key elements of culture?"

A Alright, we've determined (haven't we?) that culture is everywhere in a small business. Thus, everything that happens in an organization, from operations to administration to sales, is touched by its tentacles. Nothing escapes culture's grasp.

The way the coffee is brewed in the morning is determined by culture. So is the cleanliness of the rest rooms, the sublities of office politics, and the manner in which male and female employees coexist. Some cultural issues are more important than others, yet, when mixed together, all set the tone for a small business's success or failure.

The key elements of culture are:

- *Values.* Is there a sense of ethics, honesty, and trustworthiness overriding the way your employees deal with one another? Is the same sense of ethics, honesty, and trustworthiness apparent in the way your employees deal with your customers, vendors, and other outsiders?
- *Perception.* How does your company perceive its employees? (As its most important asset or as a necessary expense?)

  How does your company perceive its customers? (As the reason you are in business or as an interruption to the daily routine?)

  And how does your company perceive its vendors, its creditors, its shareholders, and any other outsiders? Is there a sense of mutual mission, or is there a sense of shared opposition?
- *Expense awareness.* How does your company view the almighty dollar? Is it something to be spent or something to be saved?

- *Sense of urgency.* At what pace do your employees get their work done? At a snail's pace or at a beaver's pace?
- *Time.* Do your employees respect the time of others or do they abuse it? How do they manage their own time?
- *Accountability.* Are employees held accountable for their actions? (Not just key employees—*all* employees.)
- *Follow-up.* Does your company follow up assigned missions, goals, and jobs?
- *Conflict resolution.* Is conflict resolved, or is it left to fester?

These are the key elements that make up a small business culture. They are also the key elements that make up an entrepreneur's personality.

You say you don't like your company's culture?

Guess where you must begin in order to change it?

QUESTION 69

Q "Why is the way I manage my own time a cultural issue, and what can I do to improve the way my company manages its time?"

A Let's suppose your small business's work day begins at 8:00 A.M. and you stroll in at 8:30 A.M. What message do you send to your employees?

Or let's suppose your small business's designated lunch period is one hour, and you always take an hour and a half. What message do you send to your employees?

Or let's suppose you wander into meetings ten minutes late, or let your telephone ring a half dozen times before answering it, or spend a half an hour of every day telling jokes around the Xerox machine. What messages do you send to your employees?

The manner in which the boss manages his or her time is a cultural issue because the entire company will soon be managing its time the same way. If the boss views time and the workday as a valuable and finite asset, the employees will, too. If he or she views time and the workday is as a disposable unit of measurement, the employees will, too.

Here is a sampling of the ways that small businesses who view their time as a disposable unit of measurement manage to dispose of it.

- Through meetings that don't start on time.
- Through meetings that last longer than scheduled.
- Through meetings that shouldn't have been called in the first place.
- Through a long list of telephone abuses: telephones that don't get answered on the first ring, telephone messages that don't get

acted on promptly, personal calls during business hours, callers who chat instead of getting to the point, ad infinitum and ad nauseum.

- Through people taking fifteen minutes to say what could have been said in five.
- Through waiting—for meetings, outside offices, around the water cooler, beside the fax machine, for the copy machine to warm up, inside rest rooms, for someone to get off the phone, for someone to make coffee, for . . . .

So what can the small business owner—the czar of culture, the dictator of deportment, the kaiser of conduct—do about the way his or her employees manage their time? Here are some suggestions.

- Require that employees religiously be on time. For the opening bell in the morning, for meetings, for appointments, for whatever commitments are made. (And then be on time yourself).
- Scrutinize the need for each meeting. Don't call meetings when a conversation in the office would suffice.
- Don't allow meetings to run over their allotted time.
- Train all employees, yourself included, on how to manage time. (There are consultants who specialize in this.) Then require that all employees utilize a time management system.
- Don't let gossipers gossip, joke tellers joke, or chatters chat. Deal with them. Gingerly perhaps, but deal with them.
- Train employees on the proper use of the telephone. (The phone company will do it for free.) Then set telephone standards and enforce them.
- Respect the time of visitors (i.e., customers, vendors, and other outsiders). Enact a *no wait* or *minimum wait* rule.
- Delegate. Make sure the right person is doing every job. Inefficiency is the greatest time waster of them all.

In summary, shorter and quicker is usually better. This applies to meetings, memos, and the endings of book chapters . . . .

QUESTION 70

Q "Can I change my company's culture once it's established?"

A Of course you can change your company's culture, as long as you understand that changes in culture (1) require that you make the change first, and (2) take eons to occur. Understand these two elements of the culture-changing process and change will begin whenever you wish.

Here are a collection of culture-changing tips.

- Looking for a quality-oriented culture? Become a quality freak yourself. Live it, day in and day out, for all your employees to see.

- Looking for a customer-oriented culture? Love your customers to death and long to solve their problems. Search for new ways to build longstanding relationships with them.

- Looking for a team-oriented culture? Involve everyone, exclude no one.

- Looking for a penny-pinching culture? Squeeze your pennies until they bleed. Make no exceptions, including your own office, your automobile, and your country club membership.

- Looking for a caring culture? Solve your employee's problems and watch them solve yours.

- Looking for a culture of honesty and trust? Begin at your own desk and watch it spread.

That's the way cultures are established, and that's the only way they can be changed.

PART VII

Working with Outsiders

Fact #1. Most entrepreneurs are introverts. An entrepreneurial vacuum is their favorite place to work.

Fact #2. Knowledge and experience are plentiful outside of entrepreneurial vacuums.

Fact #3. The entrepreneur who goes outside of the entrepreneurial vacuum to find knowledge and experience will achieve small business's spoils.

Outsiders—the source of knowledge and experience beyond the entrepreneurial vacuum.

QUESTION 71

Q "Should I hire consultants?"

A Why not, if they can solve your problem at a price you can afford? Solving a problem with experience beats solving it with trial and error. Anytime.

But remember, consultants are like eggs. There are good ones and there are rotten ones. Any warm body can be a consultant; they don't need an M.B.A, a Ph.D., or a high school diploma. A phone, a fax, and a few buzzwords are all that's required. Zap, zap—a consultant is born.

Besides being good or rotten, consultants are also either generalists or specialists. Generalists, are those consultants with broad business backgrounds (the best ones are ex-entrepreneurs) whose function is to determine specific problems and prescribe applicable remedies. Their tools are probing questions, exhaustive research, and a wealth of hands-on experience. The best generalists are not reluctant to pry into every nook and cranny of a small business as they put their stethoscope to its troubles before prescribing their cures.

Oftentimes those cures include the services of a follow-up consultant. Enter a specialist. Stumped with a computer issue? Hire a computer consultant. Having a quality problem? Quality consultants abound. A training issue maybe? Reach for the yellow pages. The same with sales, marketing, accounting, and human relations. There's a consultant on every streetcorner.

The trick is finding the right one . . . .

QUESTION 72

Q "How do I go about determining which consultant is best for me?"

A Carefully. Very carefully.

Hiring a consultant is not exactly like deciding which bathroom tissue to purchase. Instead, it is a gamebreaking decision with survival overtones, and the quality of the consultant you hire can be the difference between making or breaking your company. Your business wouldn't be the first to succumb from misdirection after following the bumbling advice of the wrong consultant.

And don't underestimate the cost associated with hiring the wrong consultant. The cost is not only the consultant's fee; there is also the cost of the time lost as a result of working with him or her, the cost of repairing the damages that result from poor advice, and most of all, the danger of misdirection, when your consultant leads your company in a direction that it doesn't belong.

The following are tips on how to hire, and manage, the consultant of your dreams:

- Identify your needs before beginning the search. Generalist or specialist? If specialist, specialist in what? List your criteria.
- Put the hiring #1 on your to-do list. Throw the same energy at hiring a consultant as you would at hiring a staff employee. The stakes are at least as high.
- The best way to locate the right consultant? Word of mouth. Inquire of small businesses similar to yours.
- Ask for the consultant's references, then follow them up. Leave no stone unturned when checking those references, and

remember, the best references are those the consultant *doesn't* list.

- Never hire a consultant without a resumé and credentials, no matter how inexpensive he or she may be.
- Interview more than one consultant. Have other key employees with a stake in the hire join in the interviewing process. Then compare.
- Look for chemistry between you and the consultant. The relationship between the two of you is paramount; if you can't envision the two of you working side by side ten hours a day, don't make the hire.
- Ask for a complete fee schedule up front. Tie down travel-related expenditures, per diem, and all loose financial ends.
- Make sure there is an easy and inexpensive way to end the relationship.
- Don't hesitate to send your consultant packing once you've determined the relationship isn't working. The survival of your company may be at stake.

QUESTION 73

Q "Which of the government agencies can I turn to for help?"

A What kind of help are you looking for? Resolving an operations issue? Dealing with a customer's complaint? Taking advantage of a product development opportunity? Solving a personnel problem? Forget the government agencies, those organizations are teeming with government employees and there are certain things that government employees will never understand.

Opening and operating a for-profit business is one of them.

Government agencies do play a role in small business development, however. To understand that role you must first have a working knowledge of the agencies themselves. Three warrant discussion here—the Small Business Association (SBA), the Small Business Development Centers (SBDC), and the Service Corps of Retired Executives (SCORE; not exactly a government agency but works closely with the SBA and the SBDCs).

The SBA is the most visible of the three. The SBA's purpose is to provide:

1. A liaison between small business and other government agencies. (If there is one thing that government agencies understand, it's other government agencies.)

2. Small business with a voice. Over 72,000,000 Americans either own or are employed by small business. (If 3,000,000 National Rifle Association members can move mountains, small business should at least be able to nudge hills.)

3. Assistance in locating financing. Your local SBA should have a listing of local resources available to small businesses. They can also be a last resort option for financing.

4. Assistance in procuring government contracts.

5. Seminars and workshops on small business subjects.

SBDCs are a network of local agencies (in most midsized to large cities) and are usually operated by colleges or universities. SBDC staffing comes from a variety of governmental and educational backgrounds. The SBDC's intent is to provide assistance through counseling, planning, seminars, training, networking opportunities, and access to information (libraries, for example).

SCORE is a volunteer group of (usually) ex-corporate executives (see Question 74).

The bottom line? The SBA and the SBDC can be of assistance if you're looking for the kind of help that government agencies are capable of providing. Don't look for them to solve specific problems, but rather look for them to provide networking opportunities or information that will allow you to solve those problems yourself.

The best thing those government agencies could do?

Convince their employer to leave us alone.

QUESTION 74

Q "Can the SCORE organization (Service Corps of Retired Executives) help me solve my problems?"

A That depends . . . on what your problems are and who your SCORE advisor turns out to be.

You say you're on the outside of this vocation looking inside? Trying to measure the upsides and downsides of a small business career, trying to balance its risks with its rewards, trying to determine whether or not to take the plunge? Then look no further, SCORE's advisors have been well trained to answer your questions, and are at their best at this stage of the process. Wannabe entrepreneurs are right up their alley.

You say you own an existing small business and are suffering through its typical ailments? Well, maybe your local SCORE chapter can help and maybe it can't. That will depend on the advisor assigned to you. Let's say you have a mechanical engineering problem and SCORE happens to have a mechanical engineer on its staff. Or maybe you've got a sexual harassment issue and SCORE has a qualified human relations person available. Or perhaps an impending legal problem is puzzling you and SCORE has an ex-corporate attorney on its staff. Assuming the two of you are matched, you're in luck.

On the other hand, maybe your business doesn't have a specific ailment. Perhaps it's got the small business equivalent of the flu; you know, a fever, a runny nose, and a headache. No specialist required here, just an old-fashioned general practitioner. A grizzled veteran who has seen and done it all, where small business ailments are concerned anyway. Someone who has prepared his own business plan, met his own payroll, and signed his own personal guarantee.

Well, that person, I'm sorry to say, will probably not be the person SCORE assigns to you.

That's because the RE in SCORE stands for "Retired Executives," and the majority of SCORE's members are ex-Fortune 500 employees, whose experience is in specific career fields; career fields which do not include Small Business 101. The vast majority of these folks have not written their own business plans, have not met their own payrolls, and have not signed so much as one personal guarantee.

After all, it only makes sense. We small business types couldn't tell them how to manage their complicated careers; they'll have a hard time telling us how to manage ours.

I'm not knocking the SCORE organization (I happen to be a member), I'm only pointing out its limitations, given its complement of "retired executives." After all, their intentions are good and it is a nationwide volunteering concept whose time has come. What this country really needs, however (besides a five cent cigar), is a SCORE organization made up of its current staff of "retired executives," working in conjunction with equal numbers of "retired entrepreneurs," "active entrepreneurs," and yes, even "active executives." Now there's a dream team that could make a difference.

Until this dream team concept becomes a reality, however (and someday it will), I suggest you give SCORE a try. After all, they have 400 chapters across the United States, are 13,000 members strong, and have a wealth of valuable experience at their command.

Besides, their services are free.

QUESTION 75

Q "Do I need a lawyer?"

A Everyone who loves lawyers, raise your hands.

Hmmmmm. Okay, everyone who *likes* lawyers, raise your hands.

Er, ah, let's take a different tack. Everyone who thinks there is a time and a place for lawyers, raise your hands.

No, not *that* time and *that* place. I'm talking about a legitimate time and place. A time and place that lawyers can be constructively employed. Such as:

- *When organizing your company.* A lawyer should be at your side to advise you on what works best for you. Sole proprietorship? C corporation? Subchapter S?
- *When enlisting shareholders.* Buy-sell agreements are a necessity whenever shareholders are involved. Also, anytime there are changes or additions to the shareholder roster, your lawyer should be involved.
- *When firing a troublesome employee.* An ounce of prevention is always worth a pound of cure. This is a litigation-crazy world.
- *When fielding calls from unfriendly lawyers.* Consult your lawyer before you do, or say, something you might regret.
- *When selling your business.* You won't believe all the bases that need covering. Only your lawyer knows.

Oh yes, by the way, lawyers don't work for the sheer joy of serving you, their customer. Here are a few tips on how to keep your legal expenses at a level somewhere below the cost of a stealth bomber.

- Look for alternatives to solving the problem. Try and negotiate the issue away. Make your lawyer the absolute last resort.

- Opt for mediation whenever possible. It's quicker and less expensive than the cumbersome judicial system.

- Ask for cost estimates of an attorney's fees up front. The estimate won't always hold up, but at least the attorney will know you're watching.

- Don't let your lawyer chat. Their meters are always running.

- Don't be intimidated by lawyers—they are *not* always right. You have logic, too. Feel free to use it in their presence.

- Keep your records organized. Don't let your lawyer shuffle your papers at $150 per hour, do it yourself (unless you're a sheik or an alderman and your time is worth more than your lawyer's).

- Make your lawyer itemize his or her bills. Your customers won't accept lump sum invoices and you shouldn't either.

These are litigious times we live in and the proliferation of lawyers is a sign of those times. Until society gets its head screwed on right, lawyers are destined to continue to multiply and prosper.

Use yours sparingly. But whenever the situation demands.

QUESTION 76

Q "How do I find a good lawyer?"

A There are two kinds of people in this world I wouldn't want to be. I wouldn't want to be a snake farmer and I wouldn't want to be a good lawyer. I wouldn't want to be a snake farmer because snakes are slimy, creepy, crawly creatures, and I wouldn't want to be a good lawyer because lawyers are, too.

No, just kidding. (Pity the poor lawyer who has to listen to all those lousy lawyer jokes.) The real reason I wouldn't want to be a good lawyer is because they must pay the price for all the bad lawyers. Making a living is tough enough without having to pay the price for someone else's mistakes.

And, make no mistake about it, there is a world of difference between good lawyers and bad lawyers. Good lawyers are (1) an integral part of the capitalistic system, (2) worth (almost) every penny they are paid, and (3) win whatever it is they are lawyering at 99 percent of the time. Meanwhile, the bad ones are a couple of notches below sand fleas. Thus, it behooves the entrepreneur to find, and hire, one of the good ones.

Here are several tips on how to find the good ones.

- *Network.* (There's that word again.) Network with other small business owners, as well as with bankers, accountants, and vendors. Small business owners, the veterans especially, have seen more lawyers than they care to admit, and most can refer you to the good ones, as well as steer you clear of the bad ones.
- *Look for chemistry.* A good lawyer-client relationship is just that. A relationship. Don't hire a lawyer you wouldn't want to take home to meet your mother.

- *Don't shop price, shop quality.*   Good lawyers win, bad lawyers lose, it's as simple as that. You've worked too hard to let shoddy advice from a slipshod lawyer take away everything you've earned. Let quality dictate your choice.
- *Ask for fee schedules.*   Don't wait until you've received the first invoice from your lawyer to have a cardiac arrest. Do it now, before you've established a relationship that might be difficult to end. (And be sure to ask for the billable hourly fees of the lawyer's various assistants, aids, and secretaries.)
- *Insist on experience.*   Make sure your lawyer has a background in small business or whatever field your needs require.
- *Verify legal standing.*   Don't hire a lawyer until you know he or she is in good legal standing. Your state bar association can provide the information you need.
- *Don't expect what you can't get.*   This is the age of specialization and there is too much for any one lawyer to know (business law, tax law, patent law, litigation, ad infinitum). Make sure your lawyer specializes in the subject you need.
- *Don't be afraid to pull the plug.* Made a bad hire? Then end it. The sooner the better.

Lawyers are like accountants. They consider themselves professionals and they work in a variety of different-sized organizations. Some work solo, some in small offices, and some in large multilocation firms.

The primary advantage of the large, multilocation firms is that they are one-stop shops. They cover everything under one roof, from sexual harassment to union arbitration, with dozens of stops in between. They are also venerable (most are old, established firms), credible, and oh yes, downright expensive. Those unused conference rooms don't come cheap.

The smaller or one-person offices, meanwhile, are more affordable and, thus, more entrepreneur friendly, but offer a more limited array of advice. Again, similar to accountants, there is a time and a place for both.

The best way I've found to work with lawyers? Not at all.

The second best way? Find a good one, establish a personal relationship, and pay his or her bills on time.

After all, lawyers can make formidable enemies, too.

QUESTION

Q "How important are accountants? How can I find the right one for me?"

A The counting of beans is a vital service to every small business owner, and no two accountants do it the same way. There are an endless number of ways to count them and an equally endless number of ways to charge for the service. Accountants, similar to bankers and lawyers, fill the role of gamebreaking outsiders, and must be selected with extreme care.

Accountants fall into three categories:

1. *The mom and pop firms.* The one- or two-person accounting firms, many of whom specialize in small business. Some may be CPAs, others college accounting majors, and others bookkeepers. All have their place.
2. *The regional firms.* Larger than the mom and pops, their favorite clients are the larger local companies that don't require national, or international, representation. Well-endowed with trained CPAs, they are capable of providing many of the consulting services that the mom and pop firms aren't.
3. *The national, and international, firms.* The Big Six, or Big Eight, or Big Howevermany accounting firms, the hallowed purveryors to the Fortune 500 crowd. (With good reason too—the Fortune 500 companies are the only ones who can afford them.)

Most start-up entrepreneurs belong in the small, but understanding, hands of the mom and pop firms. Fledgling small businesses don't need CPAs, but they do need plenty of help. And, after all, who can give that kind of help better than someone who is also a small business owner? Someone who has to answer their own telephones and make the same decisions and face the same crises day after day.

Later, as the entrepreneur's business grows and his or her accounting needs become more complex, the time will come to look for an accountant who can provide a wider range of services, a firm with plenty of CPA capability. Now the entrepreneur needs help with the more complex tasks of locating financing, financial statement analysis, and computer systems, not to mention tax advice. The accountant, at this stage in a small business's growth, is no longer simply a bean counter. The accountant is now a consultant.

Finally, as a company's needs continue to enlarge, so do the number of reasons to consider the regional or national firms. First, their signature on financial statements is more meaningful to the deep-pocketed lenders that growing companies need, and second, they provide a host of sophisticated (and expensive) consulting-type services that the mom and pops don't. There is a place for everyone in the bean-counting world.

Some tips on how to find the right accountant include the following:

- *Network.* (I'll bet you knew this one was coming.) But it's true. Your bankers, lawyers, or entrepreneurial peers will know who the good and not-so-good bean counters are. Allow them to save you the trouble of learning for yourself.
- *Interview.* Make the rounds. Check prices, philosophies, and chemistry. (Yes, your relationship with your accountant is exactly that . . . a relationship. Chemistry matters.)
- *Inventory.* Accountants, like any other business, can be prejudged by the way they look to the first-time viewer. Take a visual inventory of the way your prospective accountant conducts his or her business. Note the manner in which the telephone is answered, the rapidity with which phone calls are returned, the neatness of the offices. You can count on the fact that if the accountant's business procedures are sloppy, the services they provide will be, too.
- *Ask for, and check, references.* The same as you would do when hiring an employee, retaining a lawyer, or selecting a consultant.

• *Be aware of the law of supply and demand.*   There are more accountants on the streets than drug dealers. Feel free to be selective when making your choice.

Once you've located the right accountant, it's okay to use him or her for more than simply compiling your debits and credits at year's end. Because of the typical accountants' inside knowledge of their customer's business, and because of their exposure to other small businesses, accountants have a unique perspective of their customers that no other outsider can have. Every entrepreneur should demand their advice and input as part of the deal.

For instance (you might ask of your accountant), what, in his or her mind, are your business's comparative strengths? What are your weaknesses? In what areas is your balance sheet weak? What do you need to do to strengthen it? What balance sheet and P&L ratios need improving? Which of your P&L expenses are out of line? How do your gross margins compare to other businesses in similar industries? How does your ROS, ROE, and ROI stack up to the norm?

Only your accountant will know.

One final point on accountants. Similar to employees or any of your outside suppliers, they need to be held, well, accountable for their actions. The services they provide need to be reviewed on a regular basis, and their performance needs to be evaluated continually. And, in the event they aren't doing the job, they need to be replaced. Like any other nonperforming contractor.

Just as making the right choice of an accountant is a necessary element in every successful start-up, so keeping the right accountant is a necessary element in survival. Some accountants are capable of growing with a business, some are not.

It's up to the entrepreneur to make the distinction.

QUESTION

Q "How do I find, and keep, good vendors?"

A A good vendor is as valuable as a good customer (maybe moreso, especially for those non-manufacturing small businesses that depend on someone else's products for their livelihood). Without good vendors and the products or services they provide, it's adios to good customers. Good vendors and customer satisfaction run hand in hand.

But customer satisfaction is not the only thing that good vendors can do for you. Good vendors are also easier to live with than good customers. They are less fickle, less demanding, and generally more appreciative. And the really, truly, *good* vendors, those in tune with the times, recognize that they are in business to solve their customer's problems. Those problems are yours.

With good vendors at such a premium, it's a shame the typical entrepreneur doesn't work harder to find them and to maintain a healthy working relationship with them. Here's a collection of tips on how to do both.

- When selecting your primary vendors, include everyone in the decision-making process who is involved in using the product or service. Not just the owner, the president, or the director of purchasing, but also the employees (sales, marketing, operations, etc.) who will actually be consuming whatever the vendor vends.
- Ask for customer references before selecting a primary vendor. Check them. Carefully.
- Tour a potential vendor's physical facility. It's amazing how much you can learn from a tour of someone else's turf. Such

observations as neatness and orderliness of facilities, friendliness and efficiency of employees, and the organization of the tour itself, can give an up-front indication of the vendor's ability to back up promises with delivery.

- Take advantage of your vendor's training programs. Good vendors offer training programs to help their customers use their products or services correctly. You and your employees should jump at the chance to avail yourselves of those training programs.

- Look for the same partnering relationship with your vendors that you pursue with your customers. The key to that relationship? Treat their representatives (sales and customer service employees) like you would want to be treated. The relationship is sure to follow.

- Ask for a financial statement from your primary vendors. After all, you're placing your trust in their hands and you need to be sure they'll be around when it counts. The really good vendors will understand; they've probably done the same thing with their primary vendors.

- Recognize that vendors are people, too. Just as employees like to be recognized and appreciated for work well done, so do vendors. Don't reserve your soul-baring letters only for complaints; save a few for *thank yous* and *well dones.* It's amazing the difference a kind word can make.

- Pay your good vendor's bills on time, and when you can't, give them plenty of advance warning. If you've been a good customer, they'll understand, and most will be willing to help you work through your problems.

- Don't cry wolf. Save your special requests for those times when you absolutely, positively need out-of-the-ordinary service. The rest of the time? Live within your vendor's delivery criteria.

The bad news where vendors are concerned? The typical small business, unlike its Fortune 500 counterpart, doesn't have the muscle or clout to demand that its vendors jump through hoops. Instead, it must rely on relationships to get special favors.

The good news? Establishing those relationships isn't a financial issue, it's a philosophical one. Treat your vendors as you'd like to be treated, and the benefits are sure to follow.

PART VIII

Learning from Others

There are two ways to learn: one is by your own trial and error and the second is by someone else's.

The first costs time and money.

Yours.

The second costs time and money, too.

Someone else's.

QUESTION 79

Q "What is a mentor? Why are they so important?"

A A mentor is a teacher, a tutor, and a trailblazer, all rolled-up into one. A mentor can also be (if the chemistry is right), the single most important individual in an entrepreneur's business life.

It oughta be a rule: *Every entrepreneur should have his or her own mentor.*

This concept of mentoring is nothing new. Our parents were mentors for most of us. Teachers were, too. Maybe even coaches. Later, for those of us who gave the Fortune 500 route a try, a mentor may have been officially assigned to us to lead us through the maze of corporate life.

Is the maze of entrepreneurial life any less complex than the Fortune 500er's life? Is it any less costly? Is it any less dangerous? Why do the big guys utilize mentors and we don't?

For most entrepreneurs, the concept of mentoring remains foreign. Or maybe it just isn't high enough on our to do list to allocate the time to find one. Whatever the reason, we have chosen to learn our lessons by doing (trial-and-erroring) instead of by watching, listening, and learning (mentoring). We've made the unconscious decision to wade through our small business world alone. No teacher, no trailblazer, no tutor, to show us the way.

Mentors are meaningful because they show us the right way, in a career filled with too many wrong ways. Wrong ways, as in costly, time-consuming, and, all too often, fatal ways.

The best mentors don't dictate; they offer choices. The best mentors don't lead; they nudge.

The best mentors are grizzled veterans. They've been there before. They know what it takes to win.

QUESTION 80

Q "How do I find, and keep, a mentor?"

A First, a question for you: "What do angels, good employees, and mentors have in common?"

Give up? All three require a large dose of perseverance and tenacity to find.

Furthermore, in each of these three instances, the reward for that perseverance and tenacity far outweighs the effort expended. Think about it, finding an angel guarantees a sufficiently financed start-up, finding good employees guarantees execution according to plan, and finding the right mentor guarantees that the marketplace will make the decision on your survival, not your mistakes.

So, are you willing to make a commitment to perseverance and tenacity in order to locate the right mentor for you? If the answer is yes, here are some additional tips on how to find, and ultimately keep, that mentor for you.

- As always, networking (word of mouth) works best in the search for a mentor. Ask your banker, your accountant, your lawyer, your neighbor, your barber, your beautician, your bookie. Somewhere out there lurks the right mentor for you.

- The mentor/entrepreneur relationship is more of a personal experience than it is a business relationship. The chemistry had better be right.

- Organization, listening, and follow-up are the keys to working successfully with a mentor. Organize every meeting with your mentor in advance (good mentors don't like to waste time), hang onto his or her every word (good mentors need to know their advice is falling on attentive ears), and follow up until you're blue in the face (good mentors need to know their advice is being acted on).

- Be ready to answer the tough questions . . . about yourself and about your business. Good mentors need quick and hard answers and won't be shy about asking for them.
- Don't sugarcoat the condition of your business or the severity of its problems. Be truthful or be history.
- Want to get rid of a good mentor? Ask him or her for money to put into your business.
- The best mentors? Always ex-entrepreneurs. People who have been there before.

And finally, beware of the mentor who promises to lead you down the path to fame and fortune. Not every Tom, Dick, or Mary is the right mentor for you. Watch out for:

- The old-timer who begins every sentence with, "I remember when. . . ."
- The new-timer who has yet to pay the price.
- The no-timer who has paid the price but has nothing to show for it.
- The corporate-timer who doesn't know a payroll from a pecan roll.

And remember, once you've become a grizzled veteran, you too can be a successful mentor. Mentoring can be as rewarding to the mentor as it is to the mentee.

So, ex-entrepreneurs, keep your eyes open. Somewhere, a lonely entrepreneur awaits.

QUESTION

Q "Do I need a board of directors or advisors?"

A Give me one good reason why you don't need a board of directors or a board of advisors. Come on, just one.

You say you don't want to answer to anyone? Sorry, but a little accountability never hurt anyone.

You say your business is so unique no one could possibly advise you on how to manage it? Sorry, but small business is generic. You've seen one, you've seen 'em all.

You say you can get all the advice you need from your employees? Sorry, but they aren't outsiders and they don't have an outsider's perspective, and besides, you sign their paychecks. How can they be objective?

You say you're a stubborn and independent cuss, and you don't have to listen to anyone if you don't want to, and you hate to follow up, and anyway you don't want to spring for lunch for five warm bodies just to listen to their hypothetical advice? Aha, now we're talking reasons. Maybe not good ones, but reasons.

Good luck. You're going to need it.

Darn right entrepreneurs need a board of directors (or advisors). Well-organized boards should be multifaceted groups of people, capable of (1) furnishing us vacuum-dwelling entrepreneurs with an unobscured glimpse of the outside world, (2) bringing experience to our otherwise barren table, and (3) providing a backboard for in-house ideas. All at the same time.

Here are a collection of ideas on how to assemble, and use, a board of directors (or advisors).

- No more than five members on your board. Scheduling is difficult enough as it is.

- Outsiders only on boards, no insiders allowed. An outsider's perspective along with his or her long-term strategic help is what you are looking for, not the tunnel vision of an insider.
- No friends or relatives, please. Friends and relatives will tell you what you *want* to hear.
- Look for someone who won't be afraid to make you sweat a little.
- Don't encourage head-nodding, encourage dissent.
- Don't be afraid to collect individual board members whose skill and experience levels are higher than yours. After all, who better to educate you?
- Balance the board. Look for sales, marketing, finance, and human resources expertise. From variety comes depth.
- Look for board members who would not be afraid to be spokespeople for your business to the outside world. Board members can, and should, be encouraged to refer potential customers.
- Board members can also be expected to help find financing or locate additional investors.
- Consider current or potential customers for your board. They can make good sounding boards for your products or services.
- Keep your board meetings strategic in focus and work hard to keep them interesting, remembering that most directors don't want to be involved in operational issues. And beware of boredom, the enemy of all productive people.
- Boards of advisors don't have to be paid (see Question 82 for the difference between a board of advisors and a board of directors). A lunch or a dinner should be enough, as long as members feel they are being listened to.
- Pay your board of directors. Modestly perhaps, but pay them—the responsibility they are assuming deserves it.
- Expect to be asked to purchase D&O insurance (liability) for your board of directors (but not for a board of advisors). D&O insurance isn't inexpensive, but it is necessary to get the best directors.
- Be honest and straightforward in your presentations to the board. Good board members will recognize B.S. when they hear it.
- Schedule your board meetings well in advance. No more than one board meeting per quarter and always schedule your annual

meetings at least six months in advance. Send out agendas at least one month before each meeting (include all necessary reference and back-up material). Give board members plenty of time and material to prepare in advance.

- Just say no to surprises. Board members don't like to make spur-of-the-moment decisions or recommendations based on surprises. Keep them informed as you go, and don't save the heart-stopping announcements for board meetings.

In an era where information and knowledge are key to success, it is foolish not to partake of the information and knowledge that a well-rounded board can offer. Besides, boards are more loyal than other pay-for-hire alternatives (such as consultants), less expensive, and more motivated to stick around for the long term.

QUESTION 82

Q "What is the difference between a board of directors and a board of advisors?"

A Plenty.

A board of directors is empowered with a fiduciary, legally enforceable responsibility to represent the shareholders of the company that employs them. Thus members of a board of directors have voting rights, must be insured against shareholder lawsuits (D&O insurance), and are almost always compensated (not meagerly, by the way).

The responsibilities of individual board members are not to be taken lightly. In the event directors are proven to have abused, neglected, or been derelict in performing their duties, they can be fined, sued, or unceremoniously tossed in jail. Or all three. Simultaneously.

A board of directors is neither inexpensive to maintain nor inconsequential in its powers. D&O insurance is stratospheric, board member compensation and their travel can be burdensome, and boards of directors have been known to limit the powers of, or even replace, the CEO that assembled them. Shareholders are a board member's ultimate employer, and good board members aren't shy about reminding the CEO of that fact.

A board of advisors on the other hand, has no fiduciary or legally responsible duties. While a board of directors represents a company's shareholders, a board of advisors represents no one, but rather serves as an advisory council to the CEO, president, or owner. A board of advisors is an informal ad hoc committee (advisably peopled by outsiders) without legal empowerment, voting rights, or, for that matter, any kind of enforceable authority. In short, a board of advisors is a committee of advice dispensers. Nothing more.

The cost of maintaining a board of advisors is significantly less than that of a board of directors. Advisors don't have to be insured, and, because they have no legal responsibilities (and thus assume no risk) advisors are willing to work for, at the most, less than directors, and at the least, nothing. Also advisors, because they have no voting powers, are no policy-making or job-holding threat to the CEO or owner who hires them.

Those who study such things estimate that 95 percent of all successful small businesses use a board of advisors while only 5 percent use a board of directors. Though I can't vouch for those statistics, I can vouch for the logic behind them.

I'll take a board of advisors, any day.

QUESTION 83

Q "What is networking?"

A We've used the term *networking* at least a half dozen times in this book already, which means the word is getting old, at least for me. The chapters on consultants, bankers, accountants, lawyers, and mentors, have all elicited answers using the "N" word. There's nary an outside resource that can't be developed through the process of networking.

Our friend Webster defines the verb "network": *to develop contacts or exchange information with others.* Translating that definition into small business vernacular then, "network" becomes: *to complement our own experience by taking advantage of someone else's."*

Thus, in small business context, networking with a lawyer to find the right banker is taking advantage of that lawyer's experience. Networking with an accountant to find a new bookkeeper or CFO is taking advantage of that accountant's experience. And networking with another entrepreneur to learn how he or she controls, say, the workmen's compensation account, is taking advantage of another entrepreneur's experience. That's how networking works.

Think about it, there are no valid reasons not to network. None. Heck, networking is inexpensive (on most occasions free), efficient (someone else has already made the mistake), and economical (someone else has already paid the price).

So why don't we entrepreneurs network more? Here are the three reasons most are quick to offer.

1. We don't want to take the time away from our business. After all, it's we who make things happen (or so we believe anyway),

197

and the minute we walk out the door of our business, everything grinds to a halt.

2. Our independence genes won't allow us to network. (A recent study indicates that a whopping 52 percent of today's existing entrepreneurs *don't* want any help.) See what I mean? We're the Lone Ranger, and proud of it.

3. Anyway, we have all the answers already. Hey, we've lived off those answers thus far and our heads are still above water. Why stop now?

Like I said earlier. Networking. There are no *valid* reasons not to.

QUESTION 84

Q "Where can I find the best networking opportunities?"

A The best things in life are free, or so we're told, and networking is one of the best things in life for us information-starved entrepreneurs. Here is a list of networking opportunities. The only cost is the time it takes to locate them.

- *Other entrepreneurs.* No one knows your business better than your peers. Someone who has previously been, or currently is, a part of the small business community. Some cities have self-organized peer groups of current or past entrepreneurs who meet formally or informally to discuss problems and share opportunities. Inquire of your local SCORE chapter, your chamber of commerce, the SBDC, or a college or university for information on such networking groups, or ask your local sales reps (office supply, computers, etc.) who call regularly on the small businesses in your community.

  You say your city doesn't have such a peer-group networking organization? Then start one yourself. What kind of entrepreneur are you, anyway?
- *Outsiders.* Bankers, lawyers, accountants, and other providers of services to the small business community. They have discovered it is in their best interests to ensure your survival and networking is one of the best options. Let them help.
- *Business and social organizations.* Includes everything from the Rotary to the Chamber or Commerce to the Fourth of July Crazy Days Committee. Entrepreneurs are a heat-seeking breed of people, and the closer to the center of the action, the more likely they are to be found.

- *Industry organizations.* Every industry has a national organization the purpose for which is to promote its members along with the industry itself. Small businesses are the heart of such an organization's membership, and the internal networking opportunities are endless. Contact your national organization for these opportunities.
- *Government agencies.* The SBA, SCORE, and the SBDC offer opportunities to network with other entrepreneurs. All you have to do is ask.
- *Colleges and universities.* Inquire of your local college's or university's Business school department. Most offer networking contacts and opportunities, along with a generous portion of advice.

Okay, so not all networking opportunities are free. However, the alert entrepreneurs among us have detected the need for the sharing of information, as well as the opportunities that accompany that need. Most are willing to pay a reasonable price. Here are several for-profit networking opportunities available to alert entrepreneurs.

- *Magazines.* Entrepreneur Magazine, Inc. Magazine, and Success Magazine all feature how-to and what-it's-like articles for the small business reader.
- *Cyberspace.* Each of the major cyberspace providers (America Online, Prodigy, CompuServe, AT&T, and so on) provide an on-line service for small business owners. Included are question and answer services, bulletin boards for exchange of information, and a number of chat and discussion groups, led by small business professionals. (Look for even more online services in the not-too-distant future. Cyberspace is the fastest growing information medium of them all.)
- *Small business incubators.* Incubators are collections of start-up small businesses located in the same building or geographical centers within the same town. There are over 400 incubators in the United States today, and their common objective is to help their small business tenants succeed by providing low-cost space and overhead, as well as by sharing ancillary expenses. (For the nearest incubator to you, contact the National Business Incubation Association, One President Street, Athens, OH 45701, (614) 593-4331.)

With so many small businesses in the same confines, the opportunities for networking with other entrepreneurs are endless. In addition, many incubators provide low cost consulting, accounting, and professional services, thus providing even more networking opportunities.

- *The Executive Committee (TEC).*   TEC is a San Diego-based organization providing support and advice for CEOs of companies with sales of from $5 million to $400 million. Members of TEC groups meet formally once a month to trade ideas, listen to speakers, and solve mutual problems. TEC is not inexpensive but is certainly worthwhile (I was a member for three years), especially for the CEOs of fast-growth, profitable companies.

- *Entrepreneur's Edge.* A support and advice group, also San Diego-based, Entrepreneur's Edge is designed for owners and CEOs of small businesses with sales of from $750,000 to $2,000,000.

- *The American Woman's Economic Development Corp (AWED).* AWED is a Washington D.C. organization providing technical training and business counseling for its female members.

- *The Alternative Board (TAB).*   TAB is a St. Louis-based organization of entrepreneurs formed to share experiences and learn from each other's mistakes. Membership is limited to owners or chief executives of noncompeting businesses.

The entrepreneur's tunnel-visioned independence may be a virtue when it comes to the creation of a small business, but not when it comes to building and maintaining it. Suddenly, that independence becomes a burden.

Networking is the quickest, and least expensive, way to overcome a case of entrepreneurial independence. Don't leave home without it.

PART IX

Up Close and Personal

What is an entrepreneur?

Who is an entrepreneur?

Can anyone be an entrepreneur?

Once I become a successful entrepreneur what changes do I have to make?

What happens when I don't want to be an entrepreneur any more?

Who should marry entrepreneurs? (And why would anyone want to?)

All this, and more.

QUESTION

Q "What are the personal characteristics of a successful entrepreneur?"

A The personal characteristics of a successful entrepreneur include the nerves of a brain surgeon, the energy of a ten-year-old, and the ability to fly at speeds up to 100 MPH. No, wait a minute, that's Superman.

Okay, so an entrepreneur doesn't have to wear a cape, sport an "S" on his or her chest, and be readily identifiable. To the contrary, in most cases you can't tell one entrepreneur from another. Some are MBAs and some are high school dropouts; some are introverts and some are extroverts; some are cool dudes and some are dweebs. Everyone has a chance in this game.

But all entrepreneurs, to be successful and enjoy that success, must include the following four characteristics in their bag of genetic tricks:

1. *The Urge.*   All entrepreneurs share *the urge* to make mountains out of molehills, *the urge* to create something where nothing existed before, and *the urge* to do things their way.

    The urge is usually discovered early in life. Paper routes, baby sitting jobs, and lawn mowing services are examples of kid businesses that provide early indications of an incubating entrepreneur. This incubation stage usually appears in the late grade school years and continues through high school and college.

    The urge won't wane in the formative years of the entrepreneur's business career, either. To the contrary, it will only be fueled by, rather than consummated by, growth.

The only natural enemy to *the urge* is entrepreneurial burnout. The burnout that comes from repeated failure.

2. *Intuition.*   Entrepreneuring is an equal opportunity employer. There are no SAT tests, IQ tests, or Rorshach ink blot tests to sort out the winners from losers. Lack of intelligence and/or emotional instability are not barriers to entry.

    It's too bad, however, that there isn't an intuition test included in the entrepreneur's career-entry requirements, because successful entrepreneurs make a majority of their gamebreaking decisions based on intuition. No matter how much research and logic is applied to every opportunity, there are no slam dunk solutions in the small business world. Every situation has a myriad of reasons *not to*. It's intuition that makes the ultimate call.

    Every successful entrepreneur has learned, in the course of growing his or her business, to isolate the opportunities that become available, to consider their upsides and downsides, to weigh the pros and cons, and then to juggle all of the options before making the ultimate call. That call is always weighted by intuition, and the entrepreneur who is successful will be the one who is right one heck of a lot more than 50 percent of the time.

3. *The ability to live under a cloud of debt.*   All successful entrepreneurs have survived a roller-coaster career. They have won, they have lost, they have made money, they have lost money, they have generated cash, and they have incurred debt.

    Those clouds of debt have hovered menacingly overhead . . . always there while the entrepreneur sleeps, hanging around over the weekends, lingering nearby on vacations. It's a fact, most successful entrepreneurs have, at one time or another, guaranteed a vaultfull of debt, many times in excess of his or her net worth.

    Debt avoiding antidotes include soaring profitability of the business, putting the brakes on sales growth, going public, and selling the business. Only in rare instances do these debt-avoiding antidotes make their appearance in the entrepreneur's early years. Meanwhile, he or she must learn how to adapt to the spectre of debt.

4. *Eternal optimism.*   Pick an opportunity, any opportunity. There are usually more logical reasons *not to* pursue that opportunity

than reasons *to*. It is the successful entrepreneur's role in life to consider those reasons *not to*, measure them with intuition, and then smother the opportunities that survive with a blanket of eternal optimism.

Accountants and lawyers are the naysayers and the devil's advocates of the small business world. And well they should be—they are compensated handsomely to identify and educate the entrepreneur on the long list of reasons *not to*.

Meanwhile, the entrepreneur is the creator and the doer, making his or her living by overcoming the reasons not to. And then convincing others to follow.

QUESTION 86

Q **"I don't like to take risks or to gamble. Does this mean I will never make a successful entrepreneur?"**

A Risk, Webster advises us, is a "dangerous chance." A "hazard."

Well, if Webster is correct, then I maintain that starting a business is *not* a risk. Nor is it a dangerous chance or a hazard. Rather, starting a business is an opportunity . . . an opportunity to pursue a dream, to chase a rainbow, to do things our way.

No sir, a start-up isn't a risk, a dangerous chance, or a hazard because that's our symphony we're conducting and that's us holding the baton. We pick the songs that our orchestra plays, we write the score, and we hire the musicians. And just to make sure everyone plays in the right key, we sign their checks. And if we do our job the way it is supposed to be done the music will be sweet and mellow and pleasing to the ear. If we don't, it won't.

So it is with the entrepreneur. Fate doesn't determine our destinies. We do.

For me, a *dangerous chance* is bungee-jumping, walking the streets of Miami at night, or selling Microsoft short. Those are what I call risks.

The bottom line? Risk is in the eyes of the beholder, and starting a business doesn't become a risk until after you've failed. And if starting a business is perceived as an impending risk, or if you think your idea is a dangerous chance, or if you think your dream is a hazard-in-waiting, here are a few words of hard-earned advice:

Forget it. Starting a business isn't for you.

And what about gambling?

Gambling is when the house controls the deck. Gambling is when the folks with the cash are at the mercy of the folks with the cards. Gambling is when the ball tumbles into the red and you've picked the black and there isn't a thing you can do about it. Those activities are gambling and I don't enjoy them and most successful entrepreneurs don't either.

After all, if we don't have control, we aren't having fun.

Risk taking and gambling are for roulette players, Indy car drivers, and Miami pedestrians. Risk taking and gambling are not for successful entrepreneurs.

Q "Must I make the transition from entrepreneur to manager as my company grows?"

A I am sorry to inform you that the answer is yes. Every successful entrepreneur must sooner or later make the transition to manager (usually sooner).

I am also sorry to inform you that this transition isn't fair. Many of the very things that worked for us as successful start-up entrepreneurs are working against us as our business begins growing and we start accumulating employees. Suddenly, we're being asked to perform such managerial tasks as communicating, delegating, and focusing. Suddenly, we must be patient and understanding and logical. Suddenly, we're spending our time attending meetings, dealing with problems, and resolving conflicts.

Suddenly, we're doing those things we weren't cut out to do. Those organizational-type things that pushed us away from a Fortune 500 career and into an entrepreneurial career.

And therein lies the unfairness. The job of managing is not entrepreneurially friendly.

Like it or not, as our company grows, our role begins changing. Instead of making things happen ourselves, we must now convince someone else to make them happen. Instead of spending our time with customers, we must now spend our time with employees who in turn spend *their* time with customers. Instead of moving, shaking, and doing the things we want to do, we must now teach, train, and manage those things we don't want to do.

And, make no mistake about it, the difference between a start up company with one employee and a $25 million *small* business with one hundred employees is measured in light years. No, wait, I take that back, it isn't measured in light years at all. You can't measure it. The two aren't even in the same universe.

What had better be happening as our company grows and expands is that we must be making this transition to manager at the same pace the company is growing and expanding. The faster the company's growth, the faster the need for this transition becomes. If we fall behind that growth, it will only be a matter of time before our company falls behind, too.

Making this transition to manager isn't a choice, incidentally. It's as necessary to survival as a small business's cash flow, its customers, or its employees. After all, the entrepreneur is the team leader, and if the leader doesn't keep pace, the team is sure to follow.

So what's involved in making this unfriendly transition? Funny you should ask . . . .

QUESTION 88

Q "What are some of the managerial skills I must develop as my company grows?"

A First, I've got good news for you. The word *manager* is no longer a synonym for ogre, despot, or serial killer. Instead, the word now stands for *leader, motivator,* and *cheerleader.* Yes, believe it or not, today's manager can be a warm and caring human being, similar to today's clergyman or family doctor or mother-in-law.

Yes, I am happy to report, management is no longer a dirty word.

But I've got bad news for you, too. Today's manager cannot be a free-wheeling, off-the-wall, gunslinging, human being, like too many entrepreneurs I know. Instead today's successful manager must possess a collection of managerial skills that make him or her dependable, consistent, and logical through the eyes of his or her employees. That collection includes:

1. *Focus.* The ability to concentrate on one job or one project (and only one job or project), until that job is scratched from the *to do* list forever. And since this focus should play no favorites, this *one job or one project* must include those jobs and projects that are perceived as mundane, boring, and otherwise outside of the entrepreneur's enjoyment zone.

   Remember our parent's favorite admonition when we would leave the lawn halfway mowed? "A job worth starting is worth completing," they would lecture, like their parents probably lectured them fifty years before.

   Focus is nothing new.

2. *Accountability.*   Our parents understood this one, too. No lawn mowed, no allowance given. That's accountability and account-ability works because there has to be a reason not to. There has to be a cost of nonperformance and there has to be a clear under-standing as to why nonperformance is not acceptable.

3. *Clarity.*   Employees need a foundation of understanding under-lying the decisions they make. This foundation is impossible without clarity in communications. Clarity in issues such as company mission, their own job descriptions, and the perfor-mance expected of them.

4. *Delegation.*   Leverage is the goal of today's manager and delega-tion is leverage's favorite tool. No longer is the entrepreneur the primary doer, now he or she has become the primary delegator.

   Of course, there's an element of risk when delegating, espe-cially if the employees being delegated to aren't capable of doing the job. But those employees have been hired by the person doing the delegating.

   The buck stops there.

5. *Follow-up.*   Yesterday's promises must appear on today's follow-up list, and today's promises must appear on tomorrow's follow-up calendar. Employees need to know that follow-up is as dependable as next Friday's paycheck.

   The good news? The more an employee can depend on fol-low-up, the less it will be needed.

6. *Attention to detail.*   Details kill and today's successful manager refuses to let details accumulate. The successful manager knows that management isn't just one big thing, it's a combination of a lot of little things.

7. *Other entrepreneurial unfriendly skills required of a manager:*
   • Listen first. Talk later.
   • Prefer the carrot over the stick.
   • Accept blame. Deflect credit.
   • Resolve conflict.
   • Put the shoe on the other foot.

Management is a vast, multifaceted, and underrated vocation, and the transition to it is infinitely more difficult than most entrepre-neurs anticipate. I guarantee: The transition to manager will be the toughest change the entrepreneur will ever have to make.

Q "How will I know when my company has outgrown me?"

A Don't look now, but even as you read this, the Peter Principle is gnawing away at you. It's a fact, sooner or later your job is going to outgrow you, as jobs do to us all. Pick up your local newspaper if you're looking for proof. You'll see where another politician has bitten the dust, another Fortune 500 CEO has lost his limousine, another small business has filed for Chapter 11. Heroes fall, every day.

How will you know when your job outgrows you? Your business will tell you.

- *Cash flow.* A small business's cash is always the first indication of impending trouble. Cash shortages indicate underlying problems (i.e., unhealthy accounts receivables, inventory overages, sales shortfalls, expense overruns, bad acquisitions, etc.). Each of these are management issues and each are traceable to the person at the top.
- *Balance sheet.* Key ratios will head south (see Question 28). Key ratios that reflect on the performance of the person in charge.
- *Employees.* The best ones will either leave, have their resumes at full mast, or be forming a line outside your door.
- *Customers.* Customer complaints will compound. Sales will ultimately feel the impact, while quality already has.
- *Bankers or shareholders.* Their phone calls will become more frequent, their questions more pointed.

Once your business has set the stage, along comes the most telling symptom of them all:

- *Your heart.*   Work won't be fun any more. You'll arrive at work later in the morning, you'll leave earlier in the afternoon, and the golf course will replace the office on Saturday mornings.

The good news is you're an entrepreneur, not an employee. You don't have to look over your shoulder, waiting for someone to tell you that you don't have what it takes to get the job done.

Your heart will be the first to spill the news.

QUESTION

Q "What role should the spouse play in the entrepreneur's business?"

A The relationship between a spouse and an entrepreneur is similar to the relationship between a dog and a cat. The two are certainly capable of coexisting, but the road to peace will undoubtedly be rocky and conflictive. An entrepreneur's small business, especially in its formative years, can play second fiddle to no one, spouses (and family) included.

With that relationship in mind, the spouses of entrepreneurs have two options. Those two options are to either go *all the way* or *none of the way* in their knowledge of, and relationship with, the business. (Both options are fraught with danger yet both teem with opportunity. It's up to the individuals as to which will work.)

Going *all the way* means getting deeply involved in the business. It means working the business together and knowing everything there is to know about the rise and fall of a commercial enterprise through sharing and understanding its financial statements. It means working as an employee perhaps, or maybe as a partner, or at least as a co-confidant. It means no last-minute secrets, no hair-tearing surprises, and no earth-shattering bombshells. Full disclosure is the order of the day.

And *none of the way?* None of the way means letting ignorance be your guide. It means knowing absolutely nothing about *that* business. It means getting deeply involved in something else (the PTA, the Hospital Guild, the tulip club) and letting *that* business do its thing at the same time you are doing yours. It means talking about the kids at the dinner table and not about *that* business, it means working at the community hospital and not going anywhere near *that* business, and it means worrying about your tulips surviving the freeze and not *that* business surviving the cut.

And one more point while on the subject of spouses. God help the relationship when the spouse doesn't support the entrepreneur's commitment. The relationship will be the first to go.

A closing word about children and the entrepreneur's business. Of course, it's acceptable for the entrepreneur's children to be involved in a family's small business, but beware—the process is rife with danger, especially when the business has a significant number of employees. Jealousy is sure to raise its ugly head if the entrepreneur's kids are allowed to surface too quickly.

Develop them slowly. Let them earn their apprenticeship spurs the hard way . . . working for someone else (preferably another entrepreneur). Don't bring them into the business until they've developed the necessary people and leadership skills. They'll need all they can get.

And finally, a suggestion on the subject of hiring relatives other than immediate family.

Don't.

PART X

Insightful Insights

Never discount the value of a good theory or postulation. Understanding them can play an important part in understanding the ups and downs of a small business.

Here are a collection of small business theories and postulations, a collection designed to facilitate the ups in your career while softening the downs. Each has been assimilated through experience, each has been lived and re-lived, and each has been time-tested for applicability.

QUESTION

Q "What should I do, start a business from scratch or buy an existing one?"

A That depends on the specific business you are considering buying. There are a number of factors to be considered before an intelligent decision can be reached. Those factors include:

- *The business.* Do past financial statements show the potential for a legitimate return on investment within a reasonable amount of time? Do past financial statements show the potential for positive cash flow within a reasonable amount of time? Why does the current owner want to sell? (There are always hidden agendas.) Are the business's existing problems solvable or are they beyond repair?

- *The previous owner.* How important to the success of the business is the previous owner? How badly will his or her skills be missed? Will the business lose important customers upon his or her departure? Will the previous owner remain with the business long enough to bring you up to speed?

- *You (the new owner).* Are you capable of filling the business's existing voids while you're plugging the holes created by the previous owner's departure? How much do you know about the industry? How much do you know about managing a business?

- *The purchase price.* Is the price of the business low enough to allow a fair return on investment within a reasonable amount of time? Will the resulting debt choke you?

- *The terms.* The more owner financing, the better. That's because owner financing represents money that doesn't have to be borrowed from a bank and banks are always tougher on borrowers than ex-owners. Besides, ex-owners who still have a stake in the success of their old business can be an important asset to the new owners.

    Also, the longer the repayment period, the better. A short-term need to repay principal can result in a drain on cash, thereby restricting growth. Give yourself as much time as you can negotiate. A rule of thumb is that you should be able to buy back a business (repay its debt) in five years.

If these issues can be resolved to the benefit of the prospective new owner, buying an existing small business is usually preferable to starting a business from scratch. Here are several reasons why.

- *Cash flow.* An existing small business is capable of generating positive cash flow from day one of new ownership. Not so for a start-up, however . . . it can take months, even years, for the flow of cash to come around.
- *Focus.* The entrepreneur can focus his or her energies on the nuts and bolts issues of the new business and not on those pain-in-the-posterior chores that are part of every start-up. Those details have already been done.
- *Risk.* History' is an excellent fortune teller; thus small businesses with existing track records are always more predictable, and less risky, than those without. Besides this crystal ball effect, the risk factor is also less because such things as a customer base, leases, and vendor agreements are already in place.
- *Credibility.* Customers, suppliers, and lenders are more likely to establish a relationship with an ongoing business than they are with a start-up.
- *Less expensive.* It costs less money to buy an existing business than it does to start one up. This is because many of the organizational and start-up expenses have already been paid for and written off by the existing business. Also, many of the assets that are being purchased have been significantly depreciated. (Meanwhile, the startup business has to buy them new.)

Yes, all other things being equal, buying a business is better than starting one. But remember to involve the head and not the heart when structuring the deal, and beware of making emotional decisions.

After all, if the numbers and logic don't work, the new business won't either.

QUESTION

Q "Why are *grow* or *die* the entrepreneur's only two choices?"

A Most successful entrepreneurs I know are not driven by money, power, greed, or ego. They are driven by growth. Not growth for the sake of accumulation, mind you, nor growth for the sake of power, but growth for the sake of growth.

Growth is the reason why people like Bill Gates, Sam Walton, and Ted Turner, despite net worths in the billions and employees in the tens of thousands, never can seem to get enough. Money, and the power it represents, isn't the issue with these people. Growth is the issue and growth never stops.

Thus, despite their accumulated billions, they continue to strive for more. And more. They buy new company's, introduce new products, and pursue new markets. They scratch and they claw and they change the way business is done within their niche, walking over their hapless competitors like cobblestones on the street. And sometimes it appears that their pursuit of growth borders on the fanatical (and sometimes it probably does), yet the faster they grow the more frantic their chase becomes.

Gates, Walton, and Turner have learned that every successful business, large or small, has but two choices. It can either grow or it can die; there is no in-between. Anything less than growth is stagnation, and stagnation is always a prelude to death.

This fanatical pursuit of growth, incidentally, is the primary reason why the really successful entrepreneurs view the element of change as an aphrodisiac. They thrive on it, knowing full well that without change there would be no opportunity for growth and without the opportunity for growth there would be no opportunity for them.

What does this mean to the average entrepreneur's small business? It means that the drive to grow and expand and relentlessly attack must never disappear. (And when it does, it marks the time that we will disappear.) It means we should view change as an upper, not a downer. A stimulant, not a depressant. Change should represent the new road and the status quo the old road, and new roads lead to opportunities while old roads lead to places we've already been.

Furthermore, this drive for growth is a basic and universal drive, and its tenants apply to individuals, as well as to their businesses. Thus *grow or die* applies to you and I, as well as to the world's most successful entrepreneurs. We either grow or we die, we either create opportunities or we don't, and we either welcome change or we wither in status quo's grasp.

The best thing about this option of growing or dying? No one can force the decision upon us. Not the government, not our competition, not the marketplace. We either make the choice to grow ourselves or we make the choice to die.

In the final analysis, that's what makes the grow or die option so entrepreneur-friendly. No one tells us what to do.

We grow or we die of our own volition.

QUESTION

Q "Management fads. Buzzwords or reality?"

A Management fads are like inches around the waist—you can depend on a new one every few years. For instance, here are a few of the
more popular management fads that have come down the pike over the
course of my small business career.

1. *Management by objective (MBO).* It takes an old-timer to remember this one. Used widely in the precomputer years, the basic
   components of MBO—setting and reaching goals—are still with
   us today.

2. *Quality circles.* An outgrowth of the book, *Theory Z,* this management fad encouraged the use of *quality circles.* Quality circles
   are groups or teams of employees formed for the express purpose of solving a problem or creating an opportunity.

3. *Total Quality Management (TQM).* Total Quality Management
   refers to the all-encompassing process of involving and empowering employees to increase long-term profits by increasing
   quality, increasing customer focus, and decreasing costs. A
   management catch-all if you ask me, but TQM has made its impact. And it sells.

4. *Reengineering. Process analysis* some call it. It could also be
   called *rethinking corporate structure* or *logical expense management.*
   (Or if you're looking for even more creative names for reengineering, ask some of the tens of thousands of middle managers
   whose jobs have been eliminated by it.)
   Me? I'd call reengineering *fat-cutting extraordinaire.*

5. *Empowerment.*   Refers to the process of ceding to employees more and more of the responsibilities for on-the-job decision making. Designed to make a manager out of everyone.

6. *Teams.*   Hey, what's so revolutionary about the concept of teams anyway? Two heads have always been better than one.

Well, what do you think? Buzzwords or reality?

A little of both. While the window dressing of any given fad disappears over time, the meaty elements will hang around long enough to be incorporated into the next fad. There is something good to be plucked from every fad, be it goal setting or team building or cost cutting. It's up to the entrepreneur to determine exactly what that *something good* is.

But fads are here to stay, and will continue to come and go as long as consultants and authors come and go. That's because consultants must have something revolutionary to consult about and authors must have something revolutionary to write about. After all, we of the advisory community need to perpetuate ourselves. Fads go with our turf.

So, how will you, the small business owner, know whether or not to glom on to the latest management fad?

Sorry, but there's no hard and fast rule to help you make the decision. But as a learned sage once said when asked a similar question, "You can always tell the pioneers—they're the ones with the arrows in their backs."

My advice? Don't take the arrows in the back yourself, let someone else be the target. Sit back, bide your time, and wait until the bugs get worked out of the latest fad. Then move in and pluck out the meaty stuff.

Oh yes, and while on the subject of fads, there's one we haven't discussed. . . .

QUESTION 94

Q "Why should I share my financials with my employees? They don't have the background to understand them."

A   Give me one good reason why you shouldn't share your financials with your employees? Come on, now, the Industrial Revolution has long since passed, and, like it or not, the age of empowerment and the age of information is upon us.

You say your employees don't have the background to understand your financial information? Well, that's where you come in . . . your job is to provide them with that background. This *providing* process is known as training, and if you aren't willing to provide it for your performing employees, have no fear, someone else soon will.

So, why should you share your financial information?

Because in today's fast-paced, competitive, small business environment, the employee with the most information wins. And so does the team with the most information, as well as the company with the most information. Information is knowledge in these times, and knowledge always wins.

This sharing of financial information is no original concept; it's been around for longer than George Burns. Today it's called *open-book management* by the mavens of management fads, and, who knows, it could very well be tomorrow's standard instead of today's fad.

But fad or no fad, open-book management has a common denominator with the rest of the management theories. That common denominator is the employee (or the team member, the associate, or whatever those folks on the firing line are called), and it assumes that each one of them should be capable of making many of those decisions previously reserved for management (because, after all, the employee is closer to the issues involved). In other words, open-book

228

management assumes that employees are not cogs in the machine, but rather that they *are* the machine.

Open-book management is exactly what the term implies. It is the opening of those previously hallowed books and the sharing of *all* of a business's pertinent information. This sharing, or so the assumption goes, then leads to informed employees which in turn leads to employees who care, which ultimately erupts into a team filled with employees capable of making all of the key decisions within their working environment.

The primary roadblock to this free-wheeling sharing of information is that shared information is not useful information unless it is first understood. And therein lies the rub, where most entrepreneurs are concerned anyway. For, to be understood, the background for this information must first be learned, and this learning process requires time, and lots of it. We're talking time away from the job, and that's productive time. There's a cost to it and that cost initially comes directly out of the entrepreneur's pocket.

Think about it. What other reason can you pose *not* to share your financials? You say you don't want your employees to know how much money you make? (Don't worry, they have a darn good idea already—a small business's pipelines are always full.) You say you're afraid your employees will know *too much* about *your* business? (How can they know *too much?* It's their business, too.) You say you're afraid your customers will find out how sound and profitable your business is? (That's okay, too. Today's sophisticated customers *want* to do business with sound and profitable companies.) You say you're afraid your competitors might learn some inside information about your company? (Big deal. Eastern Air Lines had access to United Air Lines inside information. A lot of good it did them.)

The ultimate goal of open-book management? That employees begin to think of themselves not as employees but as business associates. That they become a part of the decision-making process and view themselves as being responsible for everything that decision making implies. And yes (listen up, all you get-rich-quick-entrepreneurs), open-book management also preaches that those who share in the decision-making process should also share in the proceeds.

To me this idea of information-sharing, or open-book management, is just another form of doing what's best for the company. And its employees. And yes, doing what's best for the entrepreneur, too.

To me open-book management is just another word for common sense. The best management theory of them all.

QUESTION

Q *"'The customer is everything.' Is this axiom really correct?"*

A It depends on your point of view. Yes, the *customer is everything* axiom is correct from your employees' points of view. Pleasing customers (solving their problems) must be their primary goal, no matter who they are or in which department they work. From the telephone operator to the shipping clerk to the account executive:

Every small business employee's number one goal should be to solve their customer's problem.

Not so, however, for the small business owner. To him (or her) the customer is, while certainly important, by no means *everything.* What is *everything* is the company's employees. That's because, without employees (good ones, anyway), there would be no customers (good ones, anyway). Thus:

Every small business owner's number one goal should be to solve his or her employees' problems.

Once the employees' problems are solved everything else is downhill. An employee whose problems have been solved is a contented and committed employee. Contented and committed employees create and manufacture crackerjack services and extraordinary products, which in turn beget contented and committed customers. And that's how the *employee is everything* axiom works. Every time.

Think about it. Which would you rather have when starting a business? Good employees or good customers?

Why, good employees, of course. That's because, without good employees, you'll never be able to find, much less keep, good customers. Start a company with poor employees and whatever good customers you do encounter will soon be heading for the exits. Start a company with good employees and whatever good customers you encounter will soon be beating a path to your door.

What does this *customer is everything* axiom really mean? It means that the more employees you have, the more time you must spend with them, solving their problems. That time spent should include the four steps previously discussed, which are: (1) hiring, (2) training, (3) motivating, and (4) replacing when necessary.

The result? The time you spend hiring and replacing employees will solve your problems, while the time you spend training and motivating them will solve both yours and theirs.

QUESTION 96

Q "Why do salespeople make so much money? Is this the way it should be?"

A Salespeople make *so much* money for the same reason that quarterbacks and pitchers make *so much* money. Quarterbacks lead the team, pitchers strike out the competition, and salespeople represent the company to the customers of the world. Thus quarterbacks, pitchers, and salespeople are perceived as the stars of the team by the outside world. After all, they sell the tickets.

Don't believe it? Have you ever noticed when a good salesperson leaves one company and heads for its competition, that salesperson is likely to take his or her best customers along? And those departed customers will remain with that salesperson and new company as long as the product or service is at least comparable to what they were getting before. The lesson? Wherever good salespeople go, the customer is sure to follow.

This customer fickleness is proof positive that customers view companies through the presence of its representatives. Their salespeople.

Like it or not, the relationship is between the customer and the salesperson, not the CFO and the customer, or the sales manager and the customer, or even the CEO and the customer. Customers don't call CEOs when they have a problem that needs solving, they call salespeople. As a result, salespeople take the blame for the screw-ups as sure as they get the credit for jobs well done. And until such time as production superintendents, accounts payable clerks, or quality control supervisors begin making regular appearances in front of customers, this is the way the system will continue to work.

Yes, the salesperson is the eyes, ears, and resident punching bag of the company's customers. Which makes the salesperson the star of the team. A business, small, medium, or large, either keeps its customers or it loses them as a result of the relationship between the salesperson and the customer.

Is this the way it should be? Probably not. From an owner's standpoint anyway, it would be preferable (and a heck of a lot easier to explain to the rest of the employees) if all employees contributed equally and were compensated equally. Star systems are not easy to manage. They beget jealousy, foster envy, and make it difficult for non-stars to accept.

Is this the way it is? A definite yes. The star system exists in sports, in entertainment, and in small business too. Right or wrong, some employees are more important than others and, try as a good manager might, he or she will never create a playing field level enough to negate this fact as long as the rules of capitalism govern the game.

A successful small business graduate from my hometown once noted that "nothing happens until a sale is made." If this statement is correct (and I'll vouch that it is), as long as *the sale* is the driving force behind any successful business, this disparity in pay between sales and the rest of the troops will continue to exist. One of our primary duties as small business owners is to learn how to explain this fact to those who draw the short straws of the compensation system.

And learn how to live with it ourselves.

QUESTION

Q "How will small business change in the next ten years?"

A The entrepreneur's life was so much simpler 30 years ago. We pursued our neighborhood customers, we fine-tuned our locally purchased products, and we deposited the proceeds in the bank across the street. The work was difficult but uncomplicated.

Those days are gone. The pace of keeping up with change is difficult enough these days, let alone the pace of keeping up with its components. The increased demands of today's informed employees, the frantic quest for updated information, the across-the-board need for quality, and the sophistication of today's customers, all require that tomorrow's small business owner be much more of a manager than yesterday's entrepreneur ever dreamed of being. Hard work and commitment are no longer enough.

Here is a partial list of notable trends in small business that will continue to gather momentum over the next decade. The reader will note that the majority of these trends involve employees. And justifiably so, for employees are leverage and it's leverage that gets the work done.

SMALL BUSINESS TRENDS

- *Teamwork.* The trend to teamwork will continue to accelerate. Tomorrow's hiring processes will focus on identifying an individual's team skills rather than his or her individual skills. Tomorrow's organization charts will focus on organizing teams and not on placing individuals. Tomorrow's compensation plans will focus on rewarding teams, not individuals.

- *Empowerment.*   The important decisions will be moved further and further down the line—where they belong.
- *Flatter organizations.*   As empowerment grows, the need for middle management will continue to disappear. Organization charts will be flatter, as a result tomorrow's entrepreneurs will have more people working directly for them.
- *Open-book management.*   Along with empowerment comes the increased need for knowledge. An empowered employee must also be an informed employee.
- *Training.*   As the work force becomes more empowered, the need for training will continue to grow. (In order to reap, tomorrow's entrepreneur must also sow.)
- *Ownership sharing.*   The best employees will look for companies where they can share in the ownership. The use of ESOPs will continue to accelerate.
- *Networking.*   Tomorrow's winners will be the small businesses that learn to network. Owners will network with other owners, employees will network with other employees. Trial and error will give way to experience.
- *Temporary workers.*   The use of temporary workers will continue to increase. Utilization of temps allows the small business to remain lean and mean through the slow times without having to lay off its loyal and skilled employees.
- *Telecommunications.*   Telecommunications will continue to take the travel out of *being there.* Work will go where the worker is (more workers will work out of their homes). Keeping pace with telecommunication's advances will beget new career fields and will be someone's full-time chore.
- *Technology.*   Continuing advances in technology will continue to affect everything the entrepreneur does. The pace of productivity increases will quicken. Just-in-time inventory will become a necessity (if it isn't already). On-line advice will be available at the touch of an icon. The information superhighway will give mom and pop access to the same information that is available to General Motors.
- *Quality.*   As the world shrinks (thanks to telecommunications and technology), more products enter what used to be the small business's exclusive domain. The consumer is becoming accustomed to buying the best. Quality is here to stay.

In summation, the duties of a successful entrepreneur are expanding. No longer is *doing* his or her primary role. Now it is managing, training, motivating, communicating, and organizing. And yes, learning.

Learning to live with today's dizzying pace of change.

QUESTION 98

Q "Come on now, small business can't be all this difficult. What is the *real* secret to success?"

A Sorry, but there isn't just one thing that makes or breaks a small business. It's a combination of things.

If your business is soaring into the stratosphere, there's a myriad reasons why. You've hired right, and fired right, and focused right, and produced a good product (or provided a good service). Not to mention that you've planned, and strategized, and listened, and delegated, and made your employees accountable, and it goes on forever the things you've done right.

If your business is diving into the depths, there are equally as many reasons why. You've hired poorly, and haven't fired when you should, and your product (or service) isn't up to snuff. Not to mention that your employees need training, you haven't managed cash properly, you've allowed your employees to abuse one another's time, and your culture lacks accountability, and . . . .

See what I mean? Many things make the difference between winning and losing and that's a universal rule of success—it doesn't only apply to running a small business. This universal rule of success applies to everything you do, whether it's coaching a football team, raising your kids, or shuffling along the backroads of life.

And this universal rule also means there's no universal fix. It means the winner in the small business game will be the entrepreneur-turned-manager who has learned that it's all those things that make the difference. The big things and the little things and the in-between things. Not just sales. Or production. Or the paper flow system. Or efficient meetings. Or clean restrooms. Or the Yellow page ads.

It's everything.

PART XI

Lessons from the Author's Career

Spend 22 years doing the same thing and you're bound to learn several valuable lessons.

I did.

Here are several of the most valuable.

QUESTION

Q **"Okay Schell, what were the two biggest mistakes you made in your entrepreneurial career?"**

A Show me a person who has spent 22 years in the entrepreneuring game and I'll show you a body covered with scars. I'm no exception.

However, two scars stand out over all of the rest.

In first place, well ahead of the rest of the list, was my intimate relationship with the trial-and-error process. I was a textbook victim of entrepreneurial loneliness disease. I had no partner, no mentor, no board of directors, no one to learn from, and no one to lean on. As a result, I stumbled through a roller-coaster career alone, just me, the marketplace, and trial-and-error, the three of us coexisting over those thrill-packed years.

Oh, I made several half-hearted efforts to find a mentor. Twice I invited Fortune 500 friends to give the process a try, but both were good friends and weren't tough enough (on me) or knowledgeable enough (of my profession). After all, their playground hadn't been the same as mine.

Twice I tried a board of directors, too. The first time, I included only insiders but encountered too many heads nodding in unison. The second time, I included only outsiders, except that none had an entrepreneur's background and I wasn't ready to listen.

Neither my mentoring attempt nor my board of directors effort were successful, and those are prime symptoms of the entrepreneurial loneliness disease—and I had a terminal case.

My second biggest mistake? I despised details (still do). You know, all the little things that go into running a small business. The boring things, the unimportant things, the things that get in your way when you're thirsting to do whatever you consider to be the important things.

As an example, I hated the long, drawn out process of hiring. Or rather, I hated all the details that go into it—the hours spent interviewing the good prospects, as well as the bad; the reinterviewing of the good prospects and narrowing their numbers down; the following up of the facts on the resume; the checking and rechecking of personal references; and the back and forth negotiating process that is an integral part of wrapping up the hiring process.

The quicker I checked hiring off my to do list, the better, I surmised. And so, all too often, I got the employees my philosophy deserved.

And so it went with many of those what-I-considered-to-be-minor details that go along with managing a small business. I didn't enjoy fussing with paperflow systems, and quality systems, and inventory systems. I was forever leaving a string of half-finished projects and discarded details in my wake.

If only I could do it all over again.

I still wouldn't like all those details, but I'd overcome the aversion.

And hire someone who did.

QUESTION 100

Q "And the two major reasons for your success?"

A Success is no accident. It is the logical result of the excess of the things we do right over the things we do wrong. And in this vocation, there is plenty of room for both.

Me? The excess of the things I did right over the mistakes I made were largely due to two decisions I made early on in my career. Those decisions were:

1. *To give my achievers space.*

   The achievers of this world don't need direction, they need space. I gave mine the space they needed and let them do the rest.

   Sure, this granting of space is a risky decision. Grant it to more wrong employees than right ones and the results can be disastrous.

   But over the years, I was right more times than I was wrong. In the end, the space I granted to the right employees persevered over the space I granted to the wrong ones.

   In the end, I created the right environment for my achievers to win.

2. *To treat my bankers like royalty.*

   No one called their bankers more often than I. No one smothered their bankers in more information than I. No one treated their bankers better than I.

   The result? I had all the capital I needed.

   I'd call my bankers with the good news and I'd call them with the bad. I kept the surprises to an absolute minimum. I'd invite them to visit; they wouldn't have to invite themselves. I'd give them a red-carpeted tour replete with guest speaker appearances (a CFO, a sales manager, a customer). I'd prepare an outline of our meeting in advance with a copy for the banker, and he'd scribble his notes in the margins. I'd follow up our meetings with letters recapping what we'd talked about (my, how those bankers do love our commitments in writing). The next time we'd meet I'd review whatever we'd discussed in our prior meeting.

And lo and behold, my banker came to trust me. And to believe in me.

The result? I had a myriad of problems over those 22 years, but capital was never one of them.

101 QUESTION

Q **"If you had it to do all over again, what is the number one thing you'd do differently?"**

A No sweat on this one.

I'd find a mentor, before the ink on my articles of incorporation was dry.

Just think, if I'd have done that, I wouldn't have spent the next 22 years correcting a million mistakes, which means I wouldn't have burned out before my time, which means my company would still be going strong with 500 employees and the slickest ESOP plan you've ever seen.

Which means I'd be doing exactly what I was meant to do. Instead of writing about it.

Index

1996 Expo Schedule

LOS ANGELES
February 10-11, 1996
Los Angeles
Convention Center

NEW JERSEY
March 30-31, 1996
Meadowlands
Convention Center

CHICAGO
April 13-14, 1996
Rosemont
Convention Center

ATLANTA
May 18-19, 1996
Cobb County Galleria

SAN MATEO
June 8-9, 1996
San Mateo County
Expo Center

DALLAS
September
14-15, 1996
Dallas Market
Hall

NEW YORK
November
2-3, 1996
Nassau Veterans
Memorial Coliseum

PHILADELPHIA
November
16-17, 1996
South Jersey
Expo Center

FT. LAUDERDALE
December 7-8, 1996
Broward County
Convention Center

MJWE

Entrepreneur Magazine's SMALL BUSINESS EXPO

Save $5.00 when you bring this ad to any Expo.

For more information, call (800) 864-6864.